A Basic History of

THE U.S. SUPREME COURT

BERNARD SCHWARTZ

Professor of Law
New York University

THE ANVIL SERIES

under the general editorship of

LOUIS L. SNYDER

ROBERT E. KRIEGER PUBLISHING COMPANY
HUNTINGTON, NEW YORK

Original Edition 1968
Reprint Edition 1979

Printed and Published by
ROBERT E. KRIEGER PUBLISHING COMPANY, INC.
645 NEW YORK AVENUE
HUNTINGTON, NEW YORK 11743

Copyright © 1968 by
Bernard Schwartz
Reprinted by Arrangement with
D. VAN NOSTRAND COMPANY, INC.

All rights reserved. No reproduction in any form of this book, in whole or in part (except for brief quotation in critical articles or reviews), may be made without written authorization from the publisher.

Printed in the United States of America

Library of Congress Cataloging in Publication Data

Schwartz, Bernard, 1923-
   A basic history of the U.S. Supreme Court.

   Reprint of the edition published by D. Van Nostrand Co., Princeton, N.J., which was issued as 97 of An Anvil original.
   Bibliography: p.
   Includes index.
   1. United States. Supreme Court—History.   I. Title.
[KF8742.S3   1979]   347'.73'2609   78-11377
ISBN 0-88275-783-0

National Series Data Program
ISSN #0570-1062

Preface

War, according to the famous aphorism, is too important a matter to be left to the generals. The work of the Supreme Court is similarly too significant in a country such as ours to be left only to the lawyers and law professors. This is particularly true of the historical functioning of the highest tribunal. It is scarcely possible to understand American history fully without an understanding of the part played in that history by the Supreme Court. In so many cases, the decisions of the Court themselves have become a vital part of the story of the nation's development.

This volume seeks to present, in brief compass, a survey of the Supreme Court's history. As a broad account it must necessarily present an overview, focusing on essential themes rather than subsidiary details. It is hoped that such general survey will prove useful to the growing number of those who desire to learn more about the institution which plays such a vital part in the polity.

BERNARD SCHWARTZ

Table of Contents

PREFACE 3

PART I—THE SUPREME COURT

1. INTRODUCTION 9
2. THE FIRST COURT 11
3. THE MARSHALL COURT 16
4. THE TANEY COURT 27
5. DRED SCOTT, WAR, AND RECONSTRUCTION 35
6. THE FOURTEENTH AMENDMENT AND DUE PROCESS 43
7. THE COURT AND Laissez-Faire 50
8. THE NEW DEAL AND "COURT-PACKING" 57
9. JUDICIAL RESTRAINT, WAR, AND COLD WAR 63
10. THE WARREN COURT 70
11. RETROSPECT AND PROSPECT 81

PART II—READINGS

1. George Washington on Judicial Appointments, 1789 91
2. Minutes of the Supreme Court's First Sessions, 1790 95
3. The Court on Advisory Opinions, July 20 and August 8, 1793 97
4. John Marshall's Autobiographical Letter, 1827 99
5. Marbury v. Madison, 1803 104
6. Thomas Jefferson on Judicial Review, September 6, 1819 110
7. Andrew Jackson's Veto Message, 1832 113
8. Charles River Bridge v. Warren Bridge, 1837 117
9. Abraham Lincoln on the Court, 1858 and 1861 122
10. Andrew Johnson's Veto of the McCardle Act, 1868 126
11. Allgeyer v. Louisiana, 1897 129
12. Mr. Dooley on the Court, 1901 132
13. Justice Holmes, Dissenting, 1905 and 1930 136
14. F.D.R. on Court-Packing, March 9, 1937 140

15. Chief Justice Hughes in Defense of the Court, March 21, 1937	146
16. Griffin v. Illinois, 1956	150
17. Georgia Interposition Resolution, 1956	153
18. Cooper v. Aaron, 1958	159
19. Reynolds v. Sims, 1964	162
20. Justice Clark on the Court in Operation	167
21. The Court's Work, October 1965	175
22. A Justice Leaves the Court, 1962 and 1965	180
RECOMMENDED READINGS	187
INDEX	189
LIST OF ANVIL BOOKS	192

Part I
THE SUPREME COURT

CHAPTER 1

Introduction

"The history of the United States," says Charles Warren at the outset of his now-classic history of the Supreme Court, "has been written not merely in the halls of Congress, in the Executive offices and on the battlefields, but to a great extent in the chambers of the Supreme Court of the United States." The vital role played by the Court in the development of the nation is an almost inevitable result of the manner in which the basic document—the Constitution—is drafted. A constitution such as ours, drawn in so many particulars with purposed vagueness, must be given meaning through more than mechanical exegesis.

The most important cases decided by the Supreme Court have stemmed from a mere handful of skeleton phrases in the Constitution, especially the grant of Congressional power "To regulate Commerce . . . among the several States" and the prohibition against the deprivation of "life, liberty, or property, without due process of law." In clothing these wholesale phrases with meaning, the Supreme Court has been left almost completely at large. Furnished with no guide, beyond the very general language of the text, the Court has been able to give meaning to such phrases in accordance with its own policy considerations in specific cases. It is true that, however the highest Court may interpret the Constitution, it is still the Constitution which is the law—not the decisions of the Court. Yet, in most cases of consequence, the constitutional language is not so precise as to make its application automatic. On the contrary, as Chief Justice Hughes once so candidly remarked: "We are under a Constitution, but the Constitution is what the judges say it is." The federal Constitution is not a self-executing document. The *ought* laid down in 1787 must run the gantlet of judicial interpretation before it attains the practical status of an *is*. This is perhaps true of all legislation, but it is especially true of a constitution like ours, which by its very nature is much less specific and detailed than an ordinary law. Such a constitution must, in practice, be what the judges say it is.

The power peremptorily to define the Constitution is what makes the work of the Supreme Court of such consequence. To that tribunal alone, in the last analysis, is assigned the function of guarding the ark of the Constitution. Through the exercise of its constitutional role, the Court has wielded power far beyond that assumed by any other judicial body. The Supreme Court has amply proved the truth of Bishop Hoadly's celebrated 1717 observation that "Whoever hath an absolute authority to interpret written . . . laws; it is he who is truly the lawgiver to all intents and purposes and not the person who wrote . . . them."

The Supreme Court is emphatically more than the usual law court. "Scarcely any political question arises in the United States," acutely observed de Tocqueville, "that is not resolved sooner or later into a judicial question." From this point of view, the highest court is primarily a political institution, in whose keeping lies the destiny of a mighty nation. Its decrees mark the boundaries between the great departments of government; upon its action depend the proper functioning of federalism and the scope to be given to the rights of the individual. A judge on such a tribunal has an opportunity to leave his imprint upon the life of the nation as no mere master of the common law possibly could. Only a handful of men in all our history have made so manifest a mark on their own age and on ages still to come as did Chief Justice Marshall or Justice Holmes. The same cannot be said of even the greatest of modern English judges. To be a judge, endowed with all the omnipotence of justice, is certainly among life's noblest callings; but the mere common-law judge, even in a pre-eminently legal polity like that in Britain, cannot begin to compare in power and prestige with a justice of our Supreme Court. A judge who is regent over what is done in the legislative and executive branches—the *deus ex machina* who has the final word in the constitutional system—has attained one of the ultimates of human authority.

CHAPTER 2

The First Court

The Judiciary Act of 1789. Article III of the federal Constitution provides that "The judicial Power of the United States, shall be vested in one supreme Court, and in such inferior Courts as the Congress may from time to time ordain and establish." One of the principal tasks of the first Congress was to give specific content to this provision. It did so in the Judiciary Act of 1789, which laid down the basic organization of the federal judicial department—with courts of general jurisdiction, as well as intermediate appellate courts, located throughout the country, and a Supreme Court as ultimate appellate tribunal. A right of appeal to the highest Court from the state courts in cases involving federal questions was provided for.

The very first thing done by the 1789 Judiciary Act was to set up a Supreme Court consisting of a Chief Justice and five associate justices. In addition, two sessions of the Court were to be held annually "at the seat of government." The details of the high bench's jurisdiction were also laid down.

It is essential to bear in mind that though the Constitution does, as stated, provide expressly for the one Supreme Court, the Court was not given direct existence as an operating tribunal by the organic text alone. The action of Congress in the Judiciary Act was necessary to create the particular body that was to constitute the Supreme Court, and that of the President and Senate to give it the personnel which alone could make of it in fact a functioning governmental organ. (*See Reading No. 1.*) In particular, the Constitution says nothing about the Supreme Court's composition; in actual fact, the membership of the high bench has varied from six (the number at the time of its creation) to five, to seven, to nine, then to ten, then seven again, and finally to the present membership of nine.

In addition, as the Constitution is written, the legislative department may control not only the composition of the Supreme Court but also its internal organization and functioning. Congress has determined the time and place of sessions of the Court, going as far in 1801 as to change its terms so that for fourteen months, between December 1801 and February 1803, the high bench did not sit. In addition, the Congressional authority in this respect extends even to the prescription of the procedural and other rules which govern the working of the Court, as well as the jurisdiction which it may exercise.

The dependence of the Supreme Court just outlined is of basic importance in understanding the history of that tribunal. It explains much of the controversy in which the Court has been embroiled, from the time of John Marshall to Franklin D. Roosevelt's "court-packing" plan. It explains, too, why the justices have at times seemed so cautious in their approach, with periods of judicial timidity alternating with those of audacity. In the background there has always been the overriding authority of Congress over the Court's composition and functioning.

Early Weakness. On February 2, 1790, the Supreme Court met in its first public session in the Royal Exchange, at the foot of Broad Street, in New York City. (*See Reading No. 2.*) The justices were elegantly attired in black and red robes, "the elegance, gravity and neatness of which were the subject of remark and approbation with every spectator," though they had discarded what Jefferson termed "the monstrous wig which makes the English judges look like rats peeping through bunches of oakum!"

The elegance of the justices' attire could, however, scarcely serve to conceal the relative ineffectiveness of the first Supreme Court, at least by comparison with what that tribunal was later to become. To understand the Court's position, it is necessary to look at the new judicial department not through twentieth century spectacles but through the eyes of men living a decade after the Constitution went into effect. "The judiciary," wrote Hamilton in *The Federalist,* "is beyond comparison the weakest of the three departments of power." This remark was amply justified by the situation of the fledgling Supreme Court.

It is hard for us today to realize that, at the beginning at least, a seat on the supreme bench was anything but the culmination of a legal career that it has since become. John Jay, the first Chief Justice, resigned to become governor of New York (certainly a lesser position by present-day standards), and

THE FIRST COURT

Alexander Hamilton declined Jay's post, being "anxious to renew his law practice and political activities in New York." Robert Harrison turned down a place on the first Supreme Court (after having been confirmed by the Senate) to become chancellor of Maryland. The weakness of the early Supreme Court is forcibly demonstrated by the fact that, in the building of the new Capitol, that tribunal was completely overlooked and no chamber provided for it. When the seat of government was moved to Washington, the high bench crept into an undignified room in the basement beneath the Senate chamber.

Early Decisions. During its first decade, the Supreme Court decided relatively few cases. In the first three years of its existence, in fact, the Court had practically no business to transact; it was not until February 1793 that the justices decided their first case. That does not, however, mean that the justices themselves were without other arduous duties. On the contrary, the 1789 Judiciary Act had placed on the members of the highest Court the obligation of personally sitting on the circuit courts that had been set up on a territorial basis throughout the country. At a time when travel was so difficult, the imposition upon the Supreme Court justices of this circuit duty was most burdensome. In 1792 the justices united in writing to the President, with regard to "the task of holding twenty-seven Circuit Courts a year. . . . We really, sir, find the burdens laid upon us so excessive that we cannot forbear representing them in strong and explicit terms."

In the Supreme Court itself, the first important decision rendered was that in *Chisholm v. Georgia* (1793), where the Court ruled that a state could be sued by an individual in a federal court. The decision, though consistent with the original language of Article III, created such a shock of surprise that the Eleventh Amendment (prohibiting suits by individuals against states) was at once proposed and adopted. Though the immediate holding in *Chisholm v. Georgia* was thus overruled, the Court's reasoning there remains of basic importance for what it tells us about the nature of the Union. To decide the case, the Court really had to determine the crucial issue of state sovereignty. If Georgia was intended to be a sovereign state under the Constitution, it could not be sued. In deciding that Georgia was subject to suit, the Court was rejecting the claim that the state was vested with the traits of sovereignty. "As to the purposes of the Union . . . ," declared Justice Wilson, "Georgia is not a sovereign state."

Aside from *Chisholm v. Georgia,* there were no noteworthy cases decided during the Supreme Court's first decade. In many respects, indeed, the most important thing done by the early Court was its refusal to decide in advance of an actual "case" or "controversy." The very first Court felt constrained to withhold even from the Father of his Country an advisory opinion on questions Washington was most anxious to have illuminated by the highest tribunal. In 1793 the President, acting through Secretary of State Jefferson, had sent to the Supreme Court a letter asking the advice of the justices with regard to a list of questions relating to international law, which had become of importance since the outbreak of the international conflict which had grown out of the French Revolution. After the members of the high tribunal had considered the matter, Chief Justice Jay replied directly to the President in a letter which, though with due deference, firmly denied the advice sought as beyond the Court's competence to give. "Our being judges of a court in the last resort," Jay wrote, "are considerations which afford strong arguments against the propriety of our extrajudicially deciding the questions alluded to." (*See Reading No. 3.*)

Since the 1793 refusal, the Supreme Court has consistently declined to act in the absence of an actual "case" or "controversy" before it. This has been the most important limitation upon the Court's jurisdiction and has barred any decisions on what Chief Justice Taft once termed "an issue of constitutional law framed . . . for the purpose of invoking the advice of this court."

The Judiciary Act of 1801. The problem of the Supreme Court justices sitting on circuit was resolved by the Judiciary Act of 1801. Unfortunately, however, that statute was an intimate part of the controversy between the Federalists and the Jeffersonians which dominated the political scene at the turn of the century. The desirable reform of relieving the Supreme Court members of their Circuit duties was less important than the creation by the lame-duck Federalist Congress of a whole new court system, with vacancies in the new tribunals to be filled by deserving members of the defeated party. The bill was enacted into law on February 13, 1801; within two weeks President Adams had filled the new positions with Federalists; and by March 2 (two days before Jefferson took office) the Senate had confirmed the appointments. The new judges, many of whose commissions were actually filled out on the last day of Adams' term of office, were derisively known as the "midnight judges."

The newly elected Jeffersonians greeted the 1801 statute with indignation. They could scarcely concur in the Federalist attempt to entrench themselves in the life-tenure judiciary by the Midnight Judges Bill. Instead, the Jeffersonian Congress did away with what they called the "army of judges" by abolishing the new courts soon after Jefferson took office, without making any provision for the displaced judges. They did so by a simple Act of March 8, 1802, repealing the 1801 Judiciary Act and providing for the revival of the former Circuit Court system.

Lost in the partisan controversy was the desirable reform effected by the 1801 act in relieving Supreme Court justices of Circuit Court duty. Instead, the obligation of sitting on the circuits continued as a burden upon the members of the highest bench. It was only after such burden was finally removed in 1891 that the Supreme Court was able fully to assert its role as guardian of the constitutional system. Though judicial review was established in 1803, it did not really become an important practical factor in the polity until the 1890's.

The Federalists themselves bitterly attacked the 1802 repealing statute as one which, in Gouverneur Morris' characterization, "renders the judicial system manifestly defective and hazards the existence of the Constitution." The Federalist argument was, however, rejected by the Supreme Court itself in *Stuart v. Laird* (1803), in a laconic opinion which stated only that Congress had constitutional authority to establish, as they chose, such inferior tribunals as they deemed proper, and to transfer a cause from one such tribunal to another. "In this last particular," said the Court, "there are no words in the constitution to prohibit or restrain the exercise of legislative power."

CHAPTER 3

The Marshall Court

The New Chief Justice. In addition to enacting the Judiciary Act of 1801, the lame-duck Federalist government performed another action of more lasting consequence in the judicial sphere. On January 20, 1801 (only six weeks before Jefferson's inauguration), President Adams nominated John Marshall as Chief Justice. Adams himself was well aware of the cardinal significance of his choice. "My gift of John Marshall to the people of the United States," he was to say years later, "was the proudest act of my life. . . . I have given to my country a Judge, equal to a Hale, a Holt, or a Mansfield." History has amply confirmed the Adams estimate. Informed opinion today would agree that, as Justice Holmes once put it, "if American law were to be represented by a single figure, sceptic and worshipper alike would agree without dispute that the figure could be one alone, and that one, John Marshall." Indeed, Holmes goes on, "there fell to Marshall perhaps the greatest place that was ever filled by a judge."

To his contemporaries, Marshall himself may well have seemed ill-equipped for the formidable task to which he was ultimately called. One who reads the modest account of his early life in his famous autobiographical letter to Joseph Story (*see Reading No. 4*) is bound to be amazed at the meagerness of his education and training, both generally and in the law itself. His only formal schooling consisted of one year under the tuition of a clergyman and one under a tutor who resided with his family. For the rest, his learning was under the superintendence of his father, who, Marshall himself concedes, "had received a very limited education." His law study was equally rudimentary, amounting only to attendance at lectures for a mere six weeks.

The lack of formal schooling was not, however, the deficiency that it might have been in another man at another time. It must be emphasized that Marshall's was not the ordinary judicial role. As one commentator puts it, "he hit the Constitution much

THE MARSHALL COURT

as the Lord hit the chaos, at a time when everything needed creating." The need was for formative genius—for the transfiguring thought that the judge normally is not called upon to impose on society. Had Marshall been more learned in the law, he might not have performed his creative task as well as he did, for his role called for the talent and insight of a statesman capable of looking beyond the confines of strict law to the needs of a new nation entered upon the task of occupying a continent.

Strengthening the Court. We have already stressed the low prestige of the early Supreme Court. All that was to change after Marshall was appointed to its central chair. By the force of his character and soundness of his legal judgment, he was to transform the Court into a coordinate department, endowed with the ultimate authority of deciding all questions of constitutionality.

It is customary to designate a particular Supreme Court by the name of its chief. Such designation was more than formalism when Marshall presided over the Court. From the time when he first took his judicial place to his death thirty-four years later, it was emphatically *the Marshall Court* that stood at the head of the judiciary. Throughout his judicial career, Marshall's consistent aim was to use the Supreme Court to lay the constitutional foundation of an effective nation. Before this aim could be realized, the prestige and power of the high tribunal itself had to be increased, for the bench to which Marshall was first appointed could hardly hope to play the positive role in welding the new nation that the great Chief Justice conceived.

As soon as Marshall began to discharge his duties as head of the highest court, Beveridge's classic biography informs us, "he quietly began to strengthen the Supreme Court." Before Marshall, the Court followed the English practice of having opinions pronounced *seriatim* by each of the justices. The practice of having instead one opinion of the Court was begun by Marshall in the very first case decided after he became Chief Justice. The change from individual opinions to the Court opinion was admirably suited to strengthen the prestige of the fledgling Supreme Court. Marshall saw that the needed authority and dignity could be attained only if the principles the Court proclaimed were pronounced by a united tribunal. To win conclusiveness and fixity for its constructions, he strove for a Court with a single voice. How well he succeeded in this is shown by the reception accorded Justice Johnson, when the latter sought for the first time to express his own views, in a case where he disagreed with the decision of the Court. "During the rest of the Session," he plaintively affirmed in a letter to Jefferson, "I heard nothing but Lectures on the Indecency of Judges cutting at each other, and the Loss of Reputation which the Virginia appellate Court had sustained by pursuing such a course."

Marbury v. Madison. Marshall's first concern was to assert for the judicial department the powers needed to enable it to forge the constitutional bonds of a strong nation. The essential step in that direction was taken only two years after he became Chief Justice, with the 1803 decision in *Marbury v. Madison*. (*See Reading No. 5.*)

That case is now rightly considered the very keystone of the constitutional arch, for in it the Supreme Court first ruled that it possessed the authority to review the constitutionality of legislative acts. Yet when the case arose it seemed to present anything but the question of judicial review. Marbury had been appointed and confirmed as one of the "midnight judges" at the very end of the Adams Administration; his commission had been signed and sealed, but had not yet been delivered, when Jefferson took office. The new President ordered Madison, just designated as Secretary of State, to withhold the commission. Marbury then applied directly to the Supreme Court for a writ of mandamus ordering the Secretary to deliver the commission. He did so under section 13 of the Judiciary Act of 1789, which vested the highest Court with original jurisdiction to issue mandamus against federal officials.

In form, all that *Marbury v. Madison* appeared to present was the question of whether mandamus could issue in such a case against the Secretary of State. In answering it, the Supreme Court could apparently either disavow its power over the executive branch and dismiss the application, or assert such power and order the commission to be delivered. To choose the first course would have been to abdicate the essentials of "the Judicial Power" conferred by the Constitution. But the second was no more satisfactory, for while it would declare a vindication of authority to hold the executive to the law, such declaration would without a doubt remain a mere paper one. There was no way for the Court to enforce its mandate against the administration. Hence, as Marshall's biographer puts it, no matter which horn of the dilemma Marshall selected, it was hard to see how his views could escape impalement.

That Marshall was able to choose neither is perhaps the best tribute of all to his judicial statesmanship. He escaped from the dilemma by relying upon the unconstitutionality of section 13 of the Judiciary Act on the ground that, since the original jurisdiction conferred upon the Supreme Court by the Constitution was exclusive, it could not validly be enlarged by statute. Thus the Court could deny Marbury's application, not because the executive branch was above the law (Marshall's opinion, on the contrary, contains a strong repudiation of that claim) but because the Court itself did not possess the original jurisdiction to issue the writ requested.

To reach the result just stated, the Court had to rule that the statute conferring such competence was invalid and, in so doing, assert judicial power to review the constitutionality of acts of Congress. From a strategic point of view, a better case could not have been chosen for declaration of the power which has ever since been considered the palladium of the constitutional structure. Since the Court's decision denied relief, there was nothing to execute—nothing which would give rise to direct conflict with the administration. More than that, the assertion of the greatest of all judicial powers was made in a case which ostensibly denied authority to the Court. The Jeffersonians themselves found it hard to attack a decision which declined, even from the hands of Congress, jurisdiction to which the highest Court was not entitled by the Constitution.

Critique. From a historical point of view, *Marbury v. Madison* was of crucial importance as the first case establishing Supreme Court power to review constitutionality. And it was of cardinal significance that that vital power was firmly established at the outset, in terms, so firm and clear that its existence has never since been legally doubted. Had Marshall not confirmed review power in his magisterial manner, it is entirely possible that it would never have been insisted upon, for it was not until the Dred Scott case in 1857 that the authority to invalidate a federal statute was next exercised by the Supreme Court. Had Marshall not taken his stand in *Marbury v. Madison,* nearly sixty years would have passed without any question arising as to the omnipotence of Congress. After so long a period of judicial acquiescence to Congressional supremacy, it is probable that opposition to it would have been futile.

Countless commentators have pointed out the lack of originality in Marshall's holding that the judges possessed the review power. Such criticism misses the point with regard to Marshall's contribution. Of course the law laid down by Marshall was inextricably woven with that expounded by his contemporaries and predecessors. Judicial review, as an essential element of the law, was part of the legal tradition of the time, derived from both the colonial and revolutionary experience. With the appearance during the Revolution of written constitutions, the review power began to be stated in modern terms. Between the Revolution and *Marbury v. Madison,* state courts asserted or exercised the power in at least twenty cases. Marshall himself could affirm, in *Marbury v. Madison,* not that the Constitution establishes judicial review, but only that it "confirms and strengthens the principle." Soon after the Constitution went into effect, assertions of review authority were made by a number of federal judges, including members of the Supreme Court sitting on circuit. That Marshall's opinion was not radical innovation does not at all detract from its importance. Marshall's achievement in *Marbury v. Madison* may not have been transformation but only articulation, but what made it momentous was the fact that it was magisterial articulation as positive law by the highest judicial officer of the land.

Political theorists have questioned whether the assumption by the Marshall Court of the review power was justified by the Constitution or was only an act of judicial usurpation. One concerned with Supreme Court history can have no such doubts. *Marbury v. Madison* authoritatively settled the review power of the judges in a manner that has never since been questioned.

To one trained in the law, the power to decide on constitutionality is the very essence of judicial power. The authority to declare constitutionality flows naturally from the judicial duty to determine the law. One may go further and say that judicial review, as first declared in *Marbury v. Madison,* has become the *sine qua non* of our constitutional machinery: draw out this particular bolt, and the machinery falls to pieces.

Review Power over States. To hold, as did *Marbury v. Madison,* that the Supreme Court could review the constitutionality of acts of Congress is to lay down only half of the doctrine of judicial review. The power to pass on the validity of state legislation is also a necessary part of the review power if the Constitution is truly to be maintained as supreme law throughout the Union. It was in *Fletcher v. Peck* (1810) that the Supreme Court first exercised the power to hold a state law unconstitutional. In ruling that a Georgia statute violated the contract clause of the Constitution, Marshall, who delivered the opinion, declared categorically that the state could not be viewed as a single, unconnected sovereign power, upon which no other restrictions are imposed than those found in its own constitution. On the contrary, it is a member of the Union, and as such is subject to the federal Constitution, which imposes enforceable limits upon the state legislatures.

In *Fletcher v. Peck,* the Marshall Court laid the second stone in the structure of American constitutional law. Yet this was still not enough to enable the Supreme Court to maintain the Constitution as the supreme law of the land. In addition to the power to review the validity of legislative acts of both the nation and states, review power over the judgments of the state courts is also necessary. Appellate authority of the Supreme Court over state-court decisions, in order to harmonize them with the Constitution, laws, and treaties of the United States, was established in two memorable decisions by the Marshall Court. The first was rendered in *Martin v. Hunter's Lessee* (1816). That case arose out of the refusal of the highest court of Virginia to obey the mandate issued by the Supreme Court in an earlier case in which the Virginia court's decision had been reversed on the ground that it was contrary to a treaty of the United States. The Virginia judges had asserted that they were not subject to the highest bench's appellate power and that the Judiciary Act provision which "extends the appellate jurisdiction of the Supreme Court to this court, is not in pursuance of the constitution of the United States." The Supreme Court, in an opinion by Justice Story, categorically rejected the holding that it could not be vested with appellate jurisdiction over state court decisions. On the contrary, such jurisdiction was seen to be an essential element of the system of national supremacy set up by the Constitution.

Five years later, in *Cohens v. Virginia,* the holding in favor of Supreme Court review power was strongly reaffirmed. Defendants there had been convicted in a Virginia court of violating that state's law prohibiting the sale of lottery tickets. They sought a writ of error from the Supreme Court on the ground that, because the lottery in question had been authorized by an act of Congress, the state prohibitory law was invalid since it conflicted with federal law. Again it was claimed that the highest tribunal had no appellate power over the state courts. With typical force, Marshall declared that such an argument was itself contrary to the Constitution. The states, he affirmed, are not independent sovereignties; they are members of one great nation—a nation endowed by the basic document with a government competent to attain all national objects. Let the nature and objects of the Union be considered, let the great principles on which the constitutional framework rests be examined, and the result must be that the Court of the nation must be given the power of revising the decisions of local tribunals on questions which affect the nation. *Cohens v. Virginia* conclusively settled the competence of the Supreme Court to review the decisions of state courts. Since that decision, state attempts to make themselves the final arbiters in cases involving the Constitution, laws, and treaties of the United States have been foredoomed to defeat before the bar of the highest tribunal.

Chase Impeachment. With the decision in *Cohens v. Virginia,* the structure of judicial power erected by the Marshall Court was completed. The judicial authority to enforce the Constitution against both the national and state governments became an accepted part of American constitutional law. All governmental acts, whether of the nation or the states, now had to run the gantlet of review by the highest bench to determine whether they were constitutional. And that Court itself was now the veritable supreme tribunal of the land, for it was vested with the last word over the state, as well as the federal, judiciaries.

The Marshall Court did not obtain this august position without opposition, often violent, within both the national and state governments. In particular, the strengthening of the judicial department was strongly resisted by the Jeffersonian party, which was dominant in the other two departments. Jefferson was, indeed, Marshall's principal antagonist throughout his life. To the great democrat, control of the validity of governmental acts by the judges would make "the constitution . . . a mere thing of wax in the hands of the judiciary." (*See Reading No. 6.*) He never really appreciated the need for judicial review as the true safeguard of constitutional rights against the power of government.

The Jeffersonians did not confine their opposition to verbal criticism. Instead, they sought to use the weapon of impeachment to bend the judicial department to their will. Their efforts in that direction culminated in the 1805 attempt to secure the impeachment of Justice Chase, then a member of the highest court. The charges against Chase were based on his acts while on the bench and were far removed from the "high Crimes and Misdemeanors" required by the Constitution. Rather, it was generally recognized that the impeachment was political in purpose. "I perceive," wrote John Quincy Adams, "that the impeachment system is to be pursued, and the whole bench of the Supreme Court to be swept away, because their offices are wanted." The arrangements for the Chase trial were as dramatic as the event itself. The pomp of the Warren Hastings impeachment, when, says Macaulay, "the grey old walls were hung with scarlet," was still vivid in the minds of all, and perhaps in imitation, the Senate Chamber was also "fitted up in a style of appropriate elegance. . . . Benches, covered with crimson." The trial itself resulted in an acquittal, for enough senators of the Jeffersonian party were convinced by the argument of the defense—"Our property, our liberty, our lives can only be protected by independent judges"—to make the vote for conviction fall short of the constitutional majority.

The failure of the Chase impeachment was a capital event in

Supreme Court history. Had Chase been removed, it would have made impossible that independence of the Court upon which the constitutional structure rests. The Chase acquittal, as a matter of history, put an end to the danger of judicial removal on political grounds. Since 1805, though impeachment proceedings have been brought against nine other federal judges, in none of these cases was the effort to secure removal based upon political reasons.

McCulloch v. Maryland. Of the Marshall Court decisions employing judicial power to lay down the doctrinal foundations of an effective nation, two are of the greatest consequence: *McCulloch v. Maryland* and *Gibbons v. Ogden*. The first established principles essential to the very existence of the Federal Government; the second rendered effective the nation's most important substantive peacetime power.

McCulloch v. Maryland (1819) presented the Court with a fact pattern as simple as it was dramatic, involving as it did a clash of conflicting sovereignties which, in most other systems, could be resolved only by force of arms. The Second Bank of the United States had been established by Congress in 1816 to serve as a depository for federal funds and to print banknotes. Maryland had imposed a tax upon the Bank's Baltimore branch, and the case arose out of an action against the cashier of this branch for the penalties prescribed for nonpayment of the tax.

The immediate issue was that of whether the Maryland law was constitutional. To decide it, the Court had to probe into the very heart of national power under the Constitution and the relation between states and nation under the supremacy clause. The opinion first took up the question of whether Congress had the power to charter a bank. The difficulty arose from the constitutional truism that the federal government is a government only of enumerated powers, and such powers did not include that to establish a bank. But that did not end the matter, for there is nothing in the Constitution which "excludes incidental or implied powers; and which requires that everything granted shall be expressly and minutely described." On the contrary, Article I, after enumerating the specific powers conferred, authorizes Congress "To make all Laws which shall be necessary and proper for carrying into Execution the foregoing Powers."

From the necessary-and-proper clause, the Court derived the

doctrine of implied powers, which has since become a basic part of our constitutional law. If the establishment of a national bank would aid the government in its exercise of its granted powers, the authority to set one up would be implied. *McCulloch v. Maryland* thus resolved the controversy that raged in the early days of the Republic between those who favored a strict construction and those who supported a broad construction of the necessary-and-proper clause. Conclusively put to rest was the view that the clause extended only to laws which were indispensably necessary. As construed by the Court, the clause (aptly termed the "sweeping clause" at the time of the adoption of the Constitution) has been the fount and origin of vast federal authority. In truth, practically every power of the national government has been expanded in some degree by the clause.

In *McCulloch v. Maryland,* the Marshall Court construed the basic document in the grand manner, in accordance with its own dictum there that we must never forget that "it is a *constitution* we are expounding"—a living instrument that must be interpreted so as to meet the practical needs of government. By refusing to bind the nation within the literal confines of its granted powers, the Court enabled it to grow and meet governmental problems which could not have been foreseen by the Framers.

Gibbons v. Ogden. *Gibbons v. Ogden* (1824) gave the Marshall Court the opportunity to deliver the classic decision on the most important substantive power vested in the nation: "To regulate Commerce with foreign Nations, and among the several States." The need to federalize regulation of commerce had been one of the principal needs which motivated the men of 1787. Yet they were interested mainly in the negative aspects of such regulation, concerned as they were with curbing state restrictions which had oppressed and degraded national commerce. It was *Gibbons v. Ogden* which first construed the Commerce Clause in a manner enabling it to be fashioned into a formidable federal regulatory tool.

The case arose out of the invention of the steamboat by Robert Fulton. New York granted to the inventor and Livingston the exclusive right to navigate state waters by steam-propelled vessels. Ogden had secured a license from Fulton and Livingston to operate steamboats between New York and New Jersey. Gibbons started his own steamboat line between the same states in defiance of the New York-granted monopoly, though his boats were licensed to engage in the coasting trade under an act of Congress. Ogden secured an injunction in a New York court to restrain Gibbons from operating within New York waters.

The perspective of a century and a half may enable us to assert today that the issue presented in *Gibbons v. Ogden* was basically simple. Though Gibbons was operating his steamboats in violation of the New York monopoly, he was acting pursuant to a federal license. Under these circumstances, the New York monopoly law came into collision with the federal licensing law and deprived Gibbons of the right to which the federal law entitled him. If *Gibbons v. Ogden* stood only for the elementary proposition that a state law incompatible with an act of Congress must fall, that would hardly justify the decision's continuing fame. *Gibbons v. Ogden* stands as a constitutional landmark because both counsel and Court did not confine themselves to the narrow issue of conflict between state and federal law. Instead, the occasion was seized for a full-scale discussion of the scope of the commerce power.

The commerce clause vests in Congress the power "To regulate Commerce." The noun "commerce" determines the subjects to which Congressional power extends. The verb "regulate" determines the type of authority that Congress can exert. Both the noun and the verb were defined most broadly by the Marshall Court. Commerce, said Marshall, covered all intercourse—a conception comprehensive enough to include within its scope all business dealings. An equally broad view was taken on the meaning of the verb "regulate." "What is this power?" Marshall asked. "It is the power to regulate; that is, to prescribe the rule by which commerce is to be governed. This power, like all others vested in Congress is complete in itself."

As thus construed, the commerce clause was to become the source of the most important powers which the federal government exercises in time of peace. If in recent years it has become almost trite to point out how regulation from Washington has come to guard and control us from the cradle to the grave, that is true only because of the Marshall Court's emphasis at the outset upon what the Supreme Court, in our own day, has termed the embracing and penetrating nature of the commerce clause.

CHAPTER 4

The Taney Court

Marshall's Successor. The Marshall Court had transformed the Supreme Court into the vital center of the constitutional system and laid down the legal foundation of an effective national government. Under Marshall, the emphasis had been strongly in favor of federal power as against the conflicting claims of the states. Constitutional principles were molded to meet the expansionist demands of the new nation. There was an almost inevitable reaction after Marshall's death in 1835. But the basic premise of judicial sovereignty was by then an established fact. The position of the Supreme Court as ultimate arbiter of constitutional questions had become an unquestioned part of the polity. Washington's difficulty in finding men of national stature to sit on so inconsequential a tribunal was now a permanent thing of the past.

Toward the end of his life Marshall himself had looked with misgiving upon the future of the high bench. His apprehension appeared justified when, after his death, Roger B. Taney was appointed to the high bench's central chair. It was Taney who had drafted the key portions of Jackson's 1832 veto message on the bill to renew the Bank of the United States and who had carried out the President's 1833 plan for the removal of government deposits from the Bank. The veto message had questioned the very review power of the Supreme Court, asserting that its decisions "must not . . . be permitted to control the Congress or the Executive." (*See Reading No. 7.*) The choice of its author to head a bench dominated by Jacksonian Democrats appeared to presage the undoing of all that the Marshall Court had done. Wrote Daniel Webster about the Taney appointment: "Judge Story thinks the Supreme Court is *gone,* and I think so too."

To those who lived during Marshall's last days, the passing of the old order may have been something to be awaited with foreboding. The historian more than a century later can see that their fears were excessive. Even at Marshall's death, it should have been evident to the discerning observer that the doctrines of national power the great Chief Justice had espoused were bound to prevail. Contemporary admirers of the Marshall constitutional edifice might look upon Taney as the instrument chosen for its destruction. But Taney himself was not the man to preside at the liquidation of the tribunal he was called upon to head. On the contrary, the Court under Taney continued the essential thrust of constitutional development begun by Marshall and his colleagues. In fact, if we look at Taney's constitutional work, avoiding a tendency to compare his accomplishments with the colossal structure erected by his predecessor, we find it far from a mean contribution. The shadow of the Dred Scott decision, it is now generally recognized, for too long cast an unfair shadow over Taney's judicial stature.

To be sure, there was the already-noted inevitable reaction after Marshall's death; but it was not as great as has often been supposed. Chief Justice Taney may not have been as nationalistic in his beliefs as his predecessor. Yet the greater emphasis on states' rights should not obscure the continuing theme of formulation of the principles needed to insure effective operation of the Constitution.

Taney and Jacksonian Democracy. That Taney would not seek to overturn the main work of the Marshall Court should have been plain from the fact that Marshall himself had favored his successor for an earlier appointment as associate justice. But that did not prevent Marshall's supporters from bitterly condemning the appointment of the new Chief Justice. "The pure ermine of the Supreme Court," affirmed one Whig newspaper, "is sullied by the appointment of that political hack." It was soon seen, however, that the partisan condemnations were unwarranted. Henry Clay, who had led the fight against Taney's confirmation, was to say to the new Chief Justice only a few years later "that no man in the United States could have been selected, more abundantly able to wear the ermine which Chief Justice Marshall honored."

Taney is in many ways a more difficult historical subject than Marshall, for his character was much more complicated than that of his relatively straightforward predecessor. Taney, like Marshall, left an autobiographical sketch; but Taney's is longer, rambling and abstruse, and unfinished. Yet it clearly reveals the more complicated character of Marshall's successor—constantly emphasizing what Taney himself termed "this morbid sensibility." This sensibility, exaggerated perhaps by his delicate health and the fact that he was a Catholic, was to remain an essential part of the true Taney, beneath the stern façade shown to contemporaries. "I do not exactly understand why *Friday* has become the fashionable day for dinners here," he plaintively complained in an 1845 letter to his son-in-law, indicating his acute susceptibility to supposed slights at his religion.

Taney himself was the first Chief Justice to give judgment in trousers instead of the traditional knee breeches, and it has been well said that there was something of portent in this wearing of democratic garb beneath the judicial robe. For, under Taney and the new majority appointed by Jackson, the Court for the first time was influenced by the Jacksonian emphasis upon personal rights as a counterweight to the property rights so stressed by the Federalists and Whigs. Taney had been one of the foremost exponents of Jacksonian Democracy, and his years on the Court marked growing judicial concern for safeguarding of the rights of the community as opposed to property rights—of the public as opposed to private welfare. "We believe property should be held subordinate to man, and not man to property," declared a leading Jacksonian editor, "and therefore that it is always lawful to make such modifications of its constitution as the good of Humanity requires." The Supreme Court under Taney was to elevate this concept to the constitutional plane.

Community Rights. As had been the case with his great predecessor, Taney made his imprint upon the Court soon after he had been appointed. Marshall had been concerned with strengthening the powers of the fledgling nation so that it might realize its political and economic destiny. Like the Framers themselves, he stressed the need to protect property rights as the prerequisite to such realization. To Jacksonians like Taney, private property, however important, was not the be-all and end-all of social existence. "While the rights of property are sacredly guarded," declared the new Chief Justice in his very first important opinion, "we must not forget that the community also have rights, and that the happiness and well being of every citizen depends on their faithful preservation."

The opinion referred to was delivered in *Charles River Bridge v. Warren Bridge* (1837)—a case which was a *cause célèbre* in its day, both because it brought the Federalist and Jacksonian views on the place of property into sharp conflict and because stock in the corporation involved was held by Boston's leading citizens and Harvard College. (*See Reading No. 8.*)

The Charles River Bridge had been operated as a toll bridge by a corporation chartered in 1785. Its franchise had some years to run when, in 1828, Massachusetts incorporated the Warren Bridge Company to build and operate another bridge near the Charles River Bridge. The second charter provided that the new bridge would become a free bridge after a short period of time. This would, of course, destroy the business of the first bridge, and its corporate owner sued to enjoin construction of the new bridge, alleging that the contractual obligation contained in its charter had been impaired.

Taney's opinion declined to rule that there had been an invalid infringement upon the first bridge company's charter rights. The reason, according to it, was that there was no express provision in the charter making the franchise granted by it exclusive or barring the construction of a competing bridge. The basic principle, Taney affirmed, is, "That in grants by the public, nothing passes by implication." In this case the contractual obligation must be construed strictly against the grantee. As there is no express obligation not to permit a competing bridge nearby, none may be read in by implication.

The Taney opinion refused to hold that the charter to operate a toll bridge granted a monopoly in the area. Instead, the charter should be construed narrowly to preserve the rights of the community: where the rights of private property conflict with those of the community, the latter must be paramount. "The object and end of all government," Taney declared in words virtually setting forth the theme of Jacksonian democracy in the economic area, "is to promote the happiness and prosperity of the community by which it is established, and it can never be assumed that the government intended to diminish its power of accomplishing the end for which it was created." Governmental power in this respect may not be transferred, by mere implication, "to the hands of privileged corporations."

Though in form the Charles River Bridge decision was a blow to economic rights, it actually facilitated economic development. The case itself arose when the corporate form was coming into widespread use as an instrument of capitalist expansion. In the famous Dartmouth College case (1819), the Marshall Court had ruled the grants of privileges in corporate charters to be contracts and, as such, beyond impairment by government. The Marshall approach here would have meant the upholding of the first bridge company's monopoly. Such a result would have had most undesirable consequences, for it would have meant that every bridge or turnpike company was given an exclusive franchise which might not be impaired by the newer forms of transportation being developed. To read monopoly rights into existing charters would be to place modern improvements at the mercy of existing corporations and defeat the right of the community to avail itself of the benefits of scientific progress.

Corporate Expansion. Taney's opinion in the Charles River Bridge case was, as it turned out, more responsive to the needs of corporate development than the dissent of Justice Story, though the latter purported to be based squarely on the Marshall goal of protecting property rights. In another important decision, too, the Taney Court contributed directly toward commercial expansion. It did so by recognizing the existence of corporate personality beyond the borders of the state of incorporation. The industrial growth which has so altered the nature of American society would scarcely have been possible had it depended solely upon individual initiative and resources. It has been the corporate device that has enabled men to establish the pools of wealth and talent needed for the economic conquest of a continent.

It should, however, be borne in mind that the corporation is entirely a creation of law, whose very existence and legal personality has its origin in some act of the law. The corporation as a legal person was developed under precolonial English law. As such, it was recognized from the beginning in American law —especially in the classic Dartmouth College decision. But it was not until Taney's opinion in *Bank of Augusta v. Earle* (1839) that the corporate device could really be made to serve the needs of the burgeoning American economy. The decision of the lower court there had held that a corporation created in one state had no power to make a contract or to act in another state. Such ruling, in effect, limited corporations to the doing of business only in the states in which they were chartered, and would have rendered all but impossible the growth of interstate business enterprises of any consequence. The Taney opinion rejected the notion that a corporation could have no existence beyond the limits of the state in which it was chartered. On the contrary, it held that a corporation, like a natural person, might act in states where it did not reside. Comity among the states provides a warrant for the operation throughout the Union of corporations chartered in any of the states.

Bank of Augusta v. Earle was the first step in what the Supreme Court in 1894 was to term "The constant tendency of judicial decisions in modern times . . . in the direction of putting corporations upon the same footing of natural persons." This tendency has been the essential jurisprudential counterpart of the economic unfolding of the nation. Looked at this way, the Bank of Augusta decision was as nationalistic as those rendered by Marshall himself. Webster could declare, after it was rendered, that "the Supreme Court is yet sound; and much as we cherish Whig victories, yet we cherish this conservative victory more; it is a triumph of the Constitution and Union again." The fear that the constitutional edifice constructed by Marshall was to be destoryed was, in large part, dispelled.

State Regulatory Power. The emphasis on community rights, which was the basis of the already-discussed Charles River Bridge decision, is also to be seen in the decisions of the Taney Court on state regulatory power. It was essentially concern for such rights that led to articulation of the *police power*—the very basis of state authority to regulate private rights. In the 1847 License Cases, the term "police powers" was used expressly to designate "nothing more or less than the powers of government inherent in every sovereignty." It is by virtue of such power that a state may, "for the safety or convenience of trade, or for the protection of the health of its citizens," regulate the rights of property and person. Thenceforth, a principal task of the Supreme Court was to be determination of the proper balance between individual rights and the police power.

In our federal system, it is equally important that a just balance be maintained between nation and states. This has been particularly true with regard to economic regulation. Marshall, with his expansive view of the commerce clause, had perhaps tilted the scale unduly in favor of national power. Taney was unwilling to use the commerce clause as an instrument to defeat state regulatory laws. On the contrary, the Court under him raised the notion of concurrent state power over commerce to the level of accepted doctrine. More than that, a line was laid down, in *Cooley v. Board Port Wardens* (1851), to determine when such state power might legitimately be exercised. Before then, the cases assumed a dichotomy between national and state authority over commerce: in all cases either Congress must possess exclusive power or the states must be vested with coextensive, concurrent power. The Cooley decision, for the first time, expressly recognized that an either/or approach was not the only possible solution. Instead, said the Court, the question of whether there is exclusive federal power or concurrent state power depends as well upon the subjects of the power—and, in particular, upon whether they are of such a nature as to require exclusive legislation by Congress. The states may regulate unless it is imperative that the subjects of the regulation be regulated by a uniform national system. Unless the subject is such that it must be regulated uniformly from Washington alone, it may be regulated by each of the states to meet the differing needs posed by their local conditions and problems—at least unless and until Congress provides otherwise.

Federal Supremacy and Slavery. If the Taney Court was thus able to fix a balance between states and nation in the field of commercial regulation, the same was not true insofar as the basic question of sovereignty as between states and federal government was concerned. The Constitution itself makes no provision for a balance between the two centers of government, but only for a preponderance of federal power within the expansive area assigned to the nation.

Despite its willingness to sustain state authority, it is unfair to characterize the Taney Court as concerned only with states' rights. On the contrary, when state authorities acted to interfere with federal power, Taney and his colleagues were firm in upholding federal supremacy. This is shown clearly in *Ableman v. Booth* (1859), a case which, during the 1850's, excited public interest comparable to that aroused by the Dred Scott case itself. The Booth case arose out of the federal prosecution of an abolitionist newspaper editor in Milwaukee for his part in rescuing a fugitive slave from federal custody. After his conviction in a federal court for violating the Fugitive Slave Act, Booth secured a writ of habeas corpus in the Wisconsin courts on the ground that the Fugitive Slave Act was unconstitutional. A writ of error was taken to the Supreme Court, but the state court directed its clerk to make no return, declaring that its judgment in the matter was final and conclusive. In effect, the Wisconsin judges were asserting a power to nullify action taken by the federal courts. To uphold the state power thus asserted would, said Taney, "subvert the very foundations of this Government." If the states could suspend the operation of federal judicial power, "no one will suppose that a Government which has now lasted nearly seventy years, enforcing its laws by its own tribunals, and preserving the union of the States, could have lasted a single year, or fulfilled the high trusts committed to it." The Constitution itself, in its very terms, refutes the claimed state power; its language in this respect, "is too plain to admit of doubt or to need comment."

Unfortunately, the Court's decision, undoubtedly correct though it was in law, was the subject of bitter political attack. To the public, the legal issues were inextricably intertwined with the whole slavery controversy. The Republican press denounced the decision as another Dred Scott case. A bill to increase judicial salaries was defeated because, as one senator put it, the justices "had done their duty in enforcing a law obnoxious to public opinion"—the Fugitive Slave Act. It was perhaps inevitable that the Supreme Court would be dragged into the slavery controversy and its decisions denounced as partisan by extremists on both sides. By its very nature, the American system converts charged political issues such as slavery into judicial questions to be resolved by the high Court. In deciding such questions, the judges were not unnaturally predisposed in favor of existing institutions, for the law applied in courts is scarcely the proper instrument to effect fundamental changes in recognized property rights. Just as naturally, too, the justices were increasingly accused of proslavery bias, accusations which became increasingly bitter as the slavery controversy itself came closer to its inevitable resolution by force.

CHAPTER 5

Dred Scott, War, and Reconstruction

The Dred Scott Case. The involvement of the Supreme Court in the increasingly bitter slavery issue reached its culmination in the 1857 Dred Scott case and the attempt there to resolve in the judicial forum the basic controversy which promised to rend the nation asunder. The slavery question, said President Buchanan in his inaugural address a few days before the Supreme Court decision, "is a judicial question, which legitimately belongs to the Supreme Court of the United States, before whom it is now pending, and will, it is understood, be speedily and finally settled."

In the Dred Scott case the Supreme Court fell a victim to its own success. The power and prestige which had been built up under Marshall, and continued under Taney, had led men to expect too much of judicial power. The justices themselves too readily accepted the notion that judicial power could succeed where political power had failed. The Dred Scott decision seized the constitutional issue by ruling squarely on the most difficult aspect of the slavery controversy—the question of slavery in the territories. And it did so by holding that that question was one that was beyond the power of the nation itself.

Taney's opinion for the Court contained two main points. First of all, he ruled that Negroes were not and could not become citizens within the meaning of the Constitution. In addition, he rejected the claim that Scott had become a free man (and hence eligible for citizenship) by virtue of residence in a territory from which slavery had been excluded by the Missouri Compromise of 1820. This was true because "the act of Congress which prohibited a citizen from holding and owning property of this kind in the territory of the United States north of the line therein mentioned, is not warranted by the Constitution, and is therefore void."

There was more, of course, in the turgid opinion of the Chief Justice, as well as the seven other opinions rendered in the case.

But what burst with such dramatic impact was the fact that the Court had denied both the right of Negroes to be citizens and the power of Congress to interfere with slaveholding in the territories. Acquiescence in such rulings was fatal alike to the Republicans and the advocates of Popular Sovereignty. It frustrated the hopes of those who sought to confine slavery to a section that would become an ever-smaller minority in an expanding nation. It meant instead that slavery itself was a national institution and that Congress could not abolish it in the territories. In a concurring Dred Scott opinion, Justice Wayne referred to the controversies involved in the case and affirmed that "the peace and harmony of the country required the settlement of them by judicial decision." Seldom, it has been well said, has wishful thinking been so spectacularly wrong.

Dred Scott itself had two direct results—though they were exactly the contrary of those which had been intended. In the first place, the storm of abuse which burst over the majority decision cast a dark shadow over the highest bench itself. No decision in our history has done more to injure the reputation of the Supreme Court. (*See Reading No. 9.*) For the better part of a generation thereafter that tribunal was to remain in the shade, playing a diminished role in the governmental structure. From an immediate point of view, even more important was the case's effect upon the political polarization of the nation. If anything, the decision had the opposite effect from that intended by those who had hoped by means of a Supreme Court pronouncement to quell the sectional strife that threatened to destroy the Union. Far from accomplishing this goal, Dred Scott actually proved a catalyst which helped precipitate the civil conflict that soon followed.

Prize Cases. In time of war, says a famous legal maxim, the laws are silent. Such maxim applied with particular force to the Supreme Court during the Civil War. During the conflict that convulsed the nation, the Court did little more than confirm the measurers taken by the government to cope with the Southern rebellion. The only important decision rendered during the war was that in the Prize Cases (1863), which dealt with the legality of President Lincoln's proclamation in 1861 of a blockade of the Southern ports. Four ships had been captured by Union vessels enforcing the blockade and had been brought into ports to be claimed as prizes. Their owners contended that they had not been lawfully seized, since a blockade was a belligerent act, which could not be proclaimed in the absence of a state of war declared by Congress. The Supreme Court recognized that it was Lincoln's blockade proclamation that constituted the beginning of the Civil War. But could the President thus begin a war without violating what the shipowners claimed to be the "inexorable rule" that the country could be involved in war legally only by declaration of Congress?

The Court in the Prize Cases avoided a direct answer to this question by stating that the President did not, by his blockade proclamation or any other act, initiate the conflict between the states. But he was bound to accept the challenge without waiting for a Congressional declaration. Since a state of war actually existed, the President could resort to belligerent measurers to deal with it, though there had been no Congressional declaration.

The bare holding of the Prize Cases was that the President could deal with the situation after Sumter as a war and employ what belligerent measures he deemed necessary without waiting for Congress to declare war. But the implications of the decision are much broader. Under it, the President can, in fact (if not in the technical contemplation of the Constitution), initiate a war. The Prize Cases constitute a clear rejection of the doctrine that only Congress can stamp a hostile situation with the character of war and thereby authorize the legal consequences which ensue from a state of war. The language of the Court constitutes juristic justification of the many instances in our history (ranging from Jefferson's dispatch of a naval squadron to the Barbary Coast to the Vietnam conflict) in which the President has ordered belligerent measures abroad without a state of war having been declared by Congress.

Other Civil War Cases. In other decisions, too, the Supreme Court confirmed governmental action taken to cope with the conflict. From a constitutional point of view, the most difficult questions were presented by measures restricting personal liberty, notably the suspension of habeas corpus by Lincoln. The legality of such suspension, as well as the other restrictions imposed by military authorities, did not, however, come to decision before the Court at all. In 1863 Congress enacted a statute expressly authorizing the President to suspend habeas corpus "whenever, in his judgment, the public safety may require it." Other laws were passed during the war approving other extraordinary executive measures. The Supreme Court ruled that such statutes ratified Lincoln's suspension of habeas corpus, as well as the other measures covered by them. The Court thus was able to avoid the difficult constitutional issue of the President's power to take such measures on his own authority.

The key consequence of the Civil War for constitutional interpretation was that it settled the dispute between state and national power which had been until then the crucial issue. Until the Civil War the advocates of state sovereignty could, despite the uniform case-law the other way, continue to assert the temporary contractual nature of the Union. The defeat of the South meant the definitive repudiation of such assertions. And the Supreme Court confirmed such repudiation in *Texas v. White,* decided shortly after the war. The issue there was whether Texas was then a state of the Union and, as such, capable of bringing suit. Defendants contended that she was not—that, having seceded and not yet being represented in Congress, she was still out of the Union. As so presented, the case turned on the question of whether or not Texas had ever left the Union. According to the Supreme Court, that question had to be answered in the negative. As far as the law was concerned, the ordinance of secession by Texas was a nullity. Texas consequently always remained a state within the purview of the Constitution.

Texas v. White may be considered the judicial ratification of the real decision on the validity of secession which had been made at Appomattox Courthouse. If the actual outcome of the conflict had been different, the Supreme Court decision could never have been made, since the constitutional nature of the Union would have been completely altered by military power. From a legal point of view, however, the Supreme Court decision definitively settled the nature of the Union as complete, perpetual, and indissoluble—not a mere league dissoluble at the pleasure of any party. "The Constitution . . . ," declares *Texas v. White,* "looks to an indestructible Union, composed of indestructible states."

Milligan and McCardle.

The Reconstruction period represents a patent aberration in the course of American constitutional development. A portion of the nation was subjected to military government in accordance with the "conquered provinces" theory of the Radical Republicans, in violation of the Bill of Rights and other organic provisions. Yet the Supreme Court never was given the opportunity to rule on the Reconstruction Act and the measures taken under it. Generally speaking, we may say that, during Reconstruction, the Court remained in the state of recession which its Dred Scott decision had induced. Unconstitutional though much of the Reconstruction program may have been, the Supreme Court itself was unable so to rule in any of the important cases brought before it during the Reconstruction period itself.

The high bench did, however, render an important decision in the 1866 Milligan case. The decision there was recently referred to by Chief Justice Warren as a "landmark," which "established firmly the principle that when civil courts are open and operating, resort to military tribunals for the prosecution of civilians is impermissible." Yet vital though the Milligan case has been as the foundation of the wall of separation between the military and civil classes in the community, it had little immediate practical effect, since during the war the Supreme Court had refused to rule on the legality of military arrests, notably in the case of Clement Vallandigham. The holding of illegality in the similar Milligan fact pattern came over a year after the war was over. Milligan himself may have had the satisfaction of being immortalized in the *Supreme Court Reports,* but that hardly was an adequate substitute for the imprisonments suffered by Copperheads and others while the Court declined to come to grips with the constitutionality of military arrests and trials.

The Milligan decision did not prevent provision in the 1867 Reconstruction Act for military rule and trial by military commissions (of the very type which Milligan had ruled illegal) in the Southern states. Efforts to prevent the enforcement of the 1867 act, on the ground of its patent unconstitutionality, by injunction suits against the President and the Secretary of War were dismissed by the Supreme Court as not within judicial competence. Then came the case of *Ex parte McCardle,* which at first appeared to bring the legality of Congressional Reconstruction squarely before the Court. McCardle arose out of the arrest under the Reconstruction Act of a Mississippi newspaper editor. Held for a trial by military commission, he petitioned for a writ of habeas corpus, challenging the Reconstruction Act's provision which authorized military detention and trial of civilians. The writ was denied by the circuit court and an appeal was taken to the Supreme Court under a statute authorizing such appeals from circuit court decisions.

The Supreme Court unanimously decided that it had jurisdiction to hear the appeal. The case was thoroughly argued upon the merits and was taken under advisement by the justices. The Court had two years earlier decided against the wartime trial of civilians by military commission in the already discussed Milligan case, and it was widely believed that it would use the McCardle appeal to invalidate the military governments authorized by the Reconstruction Act. To avoid this danger, Congress passed a bill repealing the statute authorizing an appeal to the Supreme Court from circuit court judgments in habeas corpus cases, and prohibiting the Court's exercise of any jurisdiction on appeals which had been or which might be taken. Though his impeachment trial had already begun, President Johnson met the Congressional attack on the high tribunal with a strongly worded veto. (*See Reading No. 10.*) The bill was repassed over the Presidential negative. The McCardle case was then reargued on the question of Congressional authority to withdraw jurisdiction from the Supreme Court over a case which had already been argued on the merits. The Court unanimously ruled it no longer had any jurisdiction over the case. The effect of the statute was plain: to withdraw jurisdiction over the appeal. That being the case, the Court ruled it could no longer decide such appeal.

McCardle strickingly demonstrates the fallen state of the Supreme Court in the post-Dred Scott period. The statute had as its sole purpose the prevention of a decision by the high bench on the constitutionality of the Reconstruction Act. That law, in the pithy phrase of a contemporary press comment, "put a knife to the throat of the *McCardle* Case." The McCardle law, indeed, represents the only instance in which Congress rushed to withdraw the appellate jurisdiction of the Supreme Court for the purpose of preventing a particular decision on the constitutionality of a particular law. And the McCardle decision itself permitted the Congress to do just that. "Congress," wrote former Justice Curtis (himself the author of the celebrated Dred Scott dissent), "with the acquiescence of the country, has subdued the Supreme Court."

Legal Tender Cases. The subdued position of the Supreme Court in the Reconstruction period is also shown by its two legal tender decisions. During the Civil War Congress had been forced to make substantial changes in the currency system. In three Legal Tender Acts, it had provided for the issuance of $450 million in United States notes not backed in specie (the so-called greenbacks) and provided that such notes were to be legal tender at face value in all transactions. Though the Framers' strong distrust of paper money had led them to strike from the original constitutional draft an express Congressional power to "emit bills on the credit of the United States," it was not doubted that the doctrine of implied powers articulated in *McCulloch v. Maryland* (*Chapter 3*) authorized the federal government to issue paper obligations. The constitutional controversy arose over the Congressional power to make its paper money legal tender.

During the Civil War itself, the Supreme Court had astutely avoided deciding a case challenging the validity of the greenback laws. After the war the issue could not be avoided. In *Hepburn v. Griswold* (1870), a bare majority of the high bench ruled the Legal Tender Acts invalid. When that case was decided, the Court consisted of only seven members, who divided four to three. To deprive President Johnson of the opportunity of filling expected vacancies, Congress had passed an 1866 law providing that no vacancy of the Supreme Court was to be filled until the Court was reduced to seven members. With Grant's election, the situation was changed and an 1869 statute raised the number of justices to nine and authorized the President to appoint the necessary justices. On the very day on which the decision adverse to the government was announced in *Hepburn v. Griswold,* two new justices, Strong and Bradley, who were known to support the constitutionality of the Legal Tender Acts, were appointed.

After the new justices took their seats, the Court permitted argument again on the validity of the greenback laws. This time, in the Legal Tender Cases (1871), the Congressional power was upheld and the contrary *Hepburn v. Griswold* decision curtly overruled, with Justices Strong and Bradley, plus the Hepburn dissenters, making up the new majority. Finally putting to rest the controversy over the Congressional authority in the matter, the Court ruled that the nation's fiscal powers, viewed under the *McCulloch v. Maryland* approach, included the authority to issue paper money vested with the quality of legal tender.

To the historian, the Legal Tender Cases are less important for the actual decision than for what they tell us about the position of the Court. Historians today reject the charge that Grant packed the Court for the deliberate purpose of obtaining a reversal of *Hepburn v. Griswold*. At the same time, it is clear that for years after the Legal Tender Cases, there was strong criticism because of the coincidence of the change in constitutional interpretation with the change in Court personnel. The Court's action, asserted a contemporary newspaper comment, "will greatly aggravate the growing contempt for what has long been the most respected . . . department of our government, its Judiciary."

In addition, the legal tender decisions strikingly demonstrate the Congressional predominance over the Court in the immediate post-Civil War period. The number of Supreme Court justices was first lowered, then raised, to accomplish purely political purposes. Even if there was no specific intent to pack the Court to secure a favorable legal resolution of the greenback controversy, the eventual outcome was the same as if such intent had actually motivated the political departments.

Yet even here the picture is not entirely one-sided. The very fact that the weighty issue of legal tender was accepted as a judicial issue to be resolved by the Supreme Court is ultimately even more important than the political injury inflicted on the Court. As it turned out, the vote of one justice (however the new majority was really secured) was the supreme arbiter over a matter so crucial to the economic life of the nation.

CHAPTER 6

The Fourteenth Amendment and Due Process

The Fourteenth Amendment. If the previous chapter demonstrates Congressional predominance in the immediate postbellum period and the diminished role of the judicial department, the constitutional center of gravity was soon to shift. Paradoxically, perhaps, the principal impetus for the shift was provided by the Fourteenth Amendment, which was itself a crucial part of the Radical Reconstruction program. That amendment was intended to have two principal effects. The first was to sweep away the Dred Scott decision barring citizenship for the Negro. "All persons born or naturalized in the United States," it reads, ". . . are citizens." In addition, it was made illegal for the states to deny equal civil rights to those thus made citizens by the provision that no state was to "deprive any person of life, liberty, or property without due process of law" or to "deny to any person within its jurisdiction the equal protection of the laws."

Though the framers of the Fourteenth Amendment intended it to secure to the Negro full enjoyment of his new freedom, they used words of general, rather than merely particular, application. This has meant that the vital guarantees safeguard all persons in the community. The amendment could thus develop into a great charter for the protection of individual rights.

Before the Civil War, it was the states which were the guardians of civil liberties, and they alone could determine the extent of such rights. The Bill of Rights was binding only upon the federal government—not the states. As far as the Constitution was concerned, the states were free to encroach upon individual rights as they chose, except for the comparatively minor restrictions contained in the contract and ex post facto clauses. Now, with the adoption of the Fourteenth Amendment, all this was changed. The amendment called upon the national government to protect the citizens of a state against the state itself. Thenceforth, the safeguarding of personal and property rights was to become primarily a federal function. More than that, such safeguarding was in practice to be essentially a judicial task. Hence, the constitutional power shift that was to occur toward the end of the century, from Congress to the Supreme Court.

Corporations as Persons. With the supremacy of federal power assured by Appomattox, the Supreme Court could turn from the federal-state problem to the issues posed by burgeoning industrialism. If before the Civil War the major constitutional theme was the nation-state relationship, the dominant concern now became the relationship between government and business. The danger that state sovereignty would unduly impair the power of the nation was replaced by the danger that government would unduly impede business in its destined industrial conquest of a continent. The key constitutional provision of the new industrial era was the due process clause of the Fourteenth Amendment, which was to serve as the great charter for the protection of private enterprise. For that to happen, two important stages in interpretation were necessary. The first was the inclusion of corporations within the category of "persons' protected by the amendment. The second was the judicial construction of the due process clause as a limitation of substance as well as one of procedure.

Though commentators have questioned whether the Fourteenth Amendment was actually intended to protect corporations, the Supreme Court has consistently assumed that corporations do come within the class of "persons" protected. In *Santa Clara County v. Southern Pacific Railroad* (1886), the question of whether corporations were "persons" within the amendment's meaning was extensively briefed by counsel. At the beginning of oral argument in the case, however, Chief Justice Waite tersely announced: "The court does not wish to hear argument on the question whether the provision in the Fourteenth Amendment to the Constitution, which forbids a State to deny to any person within its jurisdiction the equal protection of the laws, applies to these corporations. We are all of the opinion that it does." Though the Court in Santa Clara wrote no opinion on the point, the Waite pronouncement definitively settled the law on the matter. Countless cases have since proceeded upon the assumption that the

Fourteenth Amendment assures corporations, as well as individuals, both due process and equal protection.

The Slaughter-House Cases. If corporations had not been included within the Fourteenth Amendment, that provision could hardly have developed into the basic charter of the new American economy. Nor could such charter have fostered the post-Civil War galloping industrialism if the due process guaranteed by the amendment had been confined to its literal import of *proper procedure*. It was the judicial importation of a substantive side into due process that made it of such significance. The development by the Supreme Court of due process as a substantive restraint was not, however, one that occurred immediately. On the contrary, the first high bench decisions under the Fourteenth Amendment manifested a restrictive attitude toward its due process clause. In the earliest cases, the Court appeared unwilling to attribute more than a procedural content to due process.

The first Supreme Court test involving the Fourteenth Amendment came in the Slaughter-House Cases (1873). The Court there adopted the limited view that the amendment was intended only to protect the Negro. That being the case, the due process clause was all but irrelevant in considering the constitutionality of a Louisiana law which conferred upon one corporation the exclusive right to slaughter livestock in New Orleans. The Court declared categorically that under no construction of that clause could the restraint imposed upon the exercise of their trade by the butchers of New Orleans be held a deprivation of property without due process. Under this interpretation, with the due process clause held inapplicable to such a case, the states were left almost as free to regulate property rights as they had been before the Civil War.

The entire Supreme Court was not, all the same, in favor of the restrictive interpretation of due process. On the contrary, in Slaughter-House Cases, four justices strongly disputed the Court's casual dismissal of the due process clause. Foremost among them was Justice Field, who delivered a vigorous dissent urging the pertinency of due process to the monopoly law there at issue. In his view, a law which prohibited a large class of citizens from following a lawful employment "does deprive them of liberty as well as property, without due process of law."

Substantive Due Process. The law on the subject was soon to be altered, and the dissent of Justice Field gradually to establish itself as the view of the Court. The starting point for such development was the case-law in the railroad field. In the famous 1877 Granger Cases, the Supreme Court upheld state power to regulate the rates of railroads and other businesses affected with a public interest—a holding, never since departed from, which has served as the basis upon which governmental regulation in this country has essentially rested. It soon came to be seen, however, that the law could not leave regulated companies defenseless against arbitrary state action fixing rates. Instead, in 1890 the Court ruled that state regulatory power is subject to substantive judicial control based upon the due process clause, and nullified a state law fixing unreasonable railroad rates. Ever since it has been recognized that the due process clause permits the courts to review the substance of rate-fixing legislation.

The Supreme Court was now ready to transform the Field conception into the law of the land. What had become the rule in railroad rate cases was to become the general rule in cases involving applications of the due process clause. Definite adoption of the Field view may be dated from *Allgeyer v. Louisiana* (1897), where, in Justice Frankfurter's words, "Mr. Justice Peckham wrote Mr. Justice Field's dissents into the opinions of the Court." (*See Reading No. 11.*) In Allgeyer, for the first time, a state law was set aside on the ground that it infringed upon the "liberty" guaranteed by the due process clause. The statute in question prohibited an individual from contracting with an out-of-state marine insurance company for the insurance of property within the state. Such law, it was held, "deprives the defendants of their liberty without due process of law."

Between the Slaughter-House Cases and *Allgeyer v. Louisiana* and its progeny lies the history of the emergence of modern large-scale industry, of the consequent public efforts at control of business, and of judicial review of such regulation. Thenceforth, all governmental action—whether federal or state—would have to pass the test of substantive due process; the substantive as well as the procedural aspect of such action would be subject to Supreme Court scrutiny.

Plessy v. Ferguson. While the due process clause was thus being developed as the principal legal safeguard of property rights, the Fourteenth Amendment was of little value to the Negro, for whose benefit the amendment had primarily been intended, until well after the period of time now under discussion. It is true that the Thirteenth Amendment did put the constitutional stamp on the demise of slavery and that the Fifteenth Amendment invalidated all state laws expressly limiting the franchise at general elections to whites. But these amendments did not prevent the South from keeping the former slave in a state of economic subjection. Nor did they automatically give the Negro the ballot. Instead, resort was had to devices like literacy tests and white primaries to avoid the intent of the Fifteenth Amendment.

Even worse was the 1896 Supreme Court decision in *Plessy v. Ferguson*. At issue there was the claim that a Louisiana statute requiring separate railroad accommodations for Negro and white passengers violated the Fourteenth Amendment's requirement of equal protection of the laws. The Court rejected the contention and held, on the contrary, that mere segregation in transportation did not violate the equal protection clause. The Court refused to accept "the assumption that the enforced separation of the two races stamps the colored race with a badge of inferiority." Under the Court's doctrine, so long as laws requiring segregation did not establish unequal facilities for the Negro, he was not denied the equal protection of the laws. As the Court more recently explained it in 1954, "Under that doctrine, equality of treatment is accorded when the races are provided substantially equal facilities, even though these facilities be separate."

Plessy v. Ferguson gave the lie to the American ideal, so eloquently stated by Justice Harlan in dissent there: "Our Constitution is color-blind, and neither knows nor tolerates classes among citizens." Upon Plessy was built the whole structure of segregation that has been at the heart of the Southern system of racial discrimination.

The Plessy ruling was based on the assertion that segregation as such does not mean discrimination; if the Negro felt discriminated against, said the Court, it was "not by reason of anything found in the act, but solely because the colored race chooses to put that construction upon it." To anyone familiar with the techniques of racial discrimination, this view is completely out of line with reality. The device of holding a group of people separate—whether by confinement of Jews to the ghetto, by exclusion of untouchables from the temple, or by segregation of the Negro—is a basic tool of discrimination. "The thin disguise of 'equal' accommodations for passengers in railroad coaches," movingly declared the Harlan dissent, "will not mislead anyone, nor atone for the wrong this day done."

Yet it was to be precisely the requirement of equality of treatment articulated in the Plessy opinion that was half a century later to provide the opening wedge for the ultimate overruling of the Plessy holding itself. But the Supreme Court emphasis on the requirement of equality was still a long way off when the Plessy case was decided. As far as achievement of the primary purpose of protecting the Negro was concerned, one must conclude that the Court had construed the Fourteenth Amendment, at the turn of the century, so that it was virtually divested of legal effect.

Insular Cases. Before we discuss the manner in which the concept of substantive due process was applied by the Supreme Court during the first part of the present century, a word should be said about the Court's handling of the constitutional aspect of the imperial interlude that arose out of the Spanish-American War.

The territorial acquisitions that were the outcome of the war with Spain posed in acute form the problem of the relationship between military conquest and the Constitution. Soon after the war ended, the question of whether government in the new territories was subject to those constitutional limitations which apply in the continental United States came before the Supreme Court. The Court dealt with that question in a series of 1901 decisions that have come to be known as the Insular Cases. They arose out of the statute providing a government for conquered Puerto Rico. Among that law's provisions were revenue sections, including one requiring certain customs duties to be paid upon goods imported into the United States from that island. It was contended that such provision was invalid as applied to citrus fruits brought in from Puerto Rico, since the island had become a part of the United States within the constitutional requirement that "all Duties, Imposts, and Excises shall be uniform throughout the United States." This, in turn, said the Court, posed the broader question of whether the provisions "of the Constitution extend of their own force to our newly acquired territories."

According to the Insular Cases, whether the Constitution follows the flag (as the problem was popularly expressed at that time) depends, in the particular case, upon the type of territory that is involved. The Court drew a distinction between so-called incorporated and unincorporated territories. The former are those territories which Congress has incorporated into and made an integral part of the United States. Without express provision by Congress, territories acquired by the nation remain unincorporated. The Court ruled further that the applicability of constitutional limitations to a given territory depends upon whether it is incorporated or unincorporated. In the former, all the constitutional rights and privileges must be accorded, with the exception of those that are manifestly applicable only within the states. But the same is not true in unincorporated territories like Puerto Rico. In them, a constitutional provision like that governing duties and imposts does not restrict governmental authority.

The Insular Cases may have been the occasion for Mr. Dooley's celebrated remark that, whether or not the Constitution followed the flag, "th' supreme coort follows th' iliction returns." (*See Reading No. 12.*) But their holding has remained the basic principle in dealing with the relationship of the Constitution to overseas territories. It was to be of particular pertinence in a later age when the United States was to become a leader of the international community. What the Supreme Court said in those cases with regard to the government provided in territories acquired as a result of the Spanish War was to apply as well to the military governments set up in conquered territory almost half a century later.

CHAPTER 7

The Court and Laissez-Faire

The Income Tax Case. Substantive due process was used by the Supreme Court for almost half a century as an instrument of laissez-faire to protect corporate enterprise from governmental restraints and restrict state interventions in the economic sphere. The development in this respect was foreshadowed by the 1895 decision in the Income Tax Case. The Court there ruled invalid the income tax law of 1894, though a similar statute had previously been upheld. The decision is explainable less in legal terms than in terms of the personal antipathies of the majority justices. Counsel depicted the income tax as "a doctrine worthy of a Jacobin Club"—the "new doctrine of this army of 60,000,000—this triumphant and tyrannical majority—who want to punish men who are rich and confiscate their property."

Such an attack upon the income tax (though, technically speaking, irrelevant) found a receptive ear in the Court. "The present assault upon capital," declared Justice Field, "is but the beginning." The income tax was part of "a war of the poor against the rich; a war constantly growing in intensity and bitterness." If the Court were to sanction the income tax law, "it will mark the hour when the sure decadence of our present government will commence." And this, it should be noted, about a law that levied a tax of 2 percent on incomes above $4,000! The decision itself was nullified by the Sixteenth Amendment. Yet the case remains as an indication of the Court's mentality with regard to governmental "assaults upon capital," for it was judges who felt that way who had at their disposal the newly fashioned tool of substantive due process.

Lochner v. New York. Due process as a substantive restraint is essentially a prohibition against arbitrary governmental action. This was the view urged in dissent by Justice Field, the original exponent of substantive due process. When the Field concept came to prevail, the test of arbitrariness was also adopted. "The Fourteenth Amendment," said Field, in 1885, this time speaking for all the justices, "undoubtedly intended . . . that there should be no arbitrary deprivation of life or liberty, or arbitrary spoliation of property." Similar statements may be found in other cases toward the end of the century. Arbitrary power, as the Supreme Court itself neatly phrased it, is not due process of law.

Arbitrary action, in the sense used by the Court, means action that is willful—depending on the will alone and not done according to reason. Under this formula, arbitrary action is synonymous with unreasonable action and due process becomes a test of reasonableness. The test received classic enunciation in *Lochner v. New York* (1905), where a state regulatory statute was at issue. According to the Court, the question in cases involving due process challenges is: "Is this a fair, reasonable, and appropriate exercise of the police power of the State, or is it an unreasonable, unnecessary, and arbitrary interference with the right of the individual?"

In Lochner the Court indicated that reasonableness under due process must be determined as an objective fact by the judge upon his own independent judgment. In holding a law prescribing maximum hours for bakers invalid, the Court substituted its judgment for that of the legislature and decided for itself that the statute was not reasonably related to any of the social ends for which governmental power might validly be exercised. The Court strongly denied that it was substituting its judgment for that of the legislature. Despite such disclaimer, substitution of the judicial for the legislative judgment was the precise thing which did occur. "This case," asserted the celebrated dissent of Justice Holmes, "is decided upon an economic theory which a large part of the country does not entertain." It was because the Court that decided the Lochner case disagreed with the economic theory upon which the legislature had acted that it struck down the statute as unreasonable.

Even in the heyday of the Lochner approach, the Court continually asserted that it was not, like the legislature itself, concerned with the wisdom and policy of legislation. But the manner in which it actually acted belied its assertion. And there were times when the true situation was acknowledged by members of the high bench themselves. "But plainly . . . ," avowed Justice

McReynolds in an important case, "this Court must have regard to the wisdom of the enactment. At least, we must inquire concerning its purpose and decide whether . . . the end is legitimate and the means appropriate." Justice Harlan on one occasion was even more candid. "I want to say to you young gentlemen," he declared in a lecture to law students, "that if we don't like an act of Congress, we don't have much trouble to find grounds for declaring it unconstitutional."

Lochner and Laissez-Faire. Judicial utilization of the Lochner approach to substantive due process meant more than mere control in the abstract of the wisdom of legislation. Court control was directed to a particular purpose—the invalidation of state laws that conflicted with the laissez-faire thinking which prevailed at the turn of the century. The Fourteenth Amendment became the rallying point for judicial resistance to efforts to control industrial excesses. "The paternal theory of government," declared Justice Brewer, one of the principal architects of the post-1890 doctrine of due process, "is to me odious. The utmost possible liberty to the individual, and the fullest possible protection to him and his property, is both the limitation and duty of government." To a Court which adopted the Brewer philosophy, the "liberty" protected by the Fourteenth Amendment became synonymous with governmental hands-off in the field of economic relations. Any legislative encroachment upon the existing economic order became suspect. "For years," the Supreme Court itself conceded in 1952, "the Court struck down social legislation when a particular law did not fit the notions of a majority of Justices as to legislation appropriate for a free enterprise system."

Lochner itself set a pattern that prevailed for a generation. During that time, the due process clause was used to invalidate a host of laws seeking to regulate economic abuses. The impact of the judicial veto is best seen from statistics: in the period between 1890 and 1937 the Supreme Court held invalid 228 state statutes.

In no way did substantive due process under the Lochner approach affect the society more than in its impact upon governmental power to protect the worker from the abuses of industrialism. Such abuses led to legislative attempts to safeguard labor by laying down minimum standards governing employment. These laws could not, however, successfully run the gantlet of the new constitutional doctrine. Governmental regulation of the relations between capital and labor was deemed a violation of the liberty of contract that was, until our own day, considered the basic part of the liberty safeguarded by the due process clause. In a series of decisions in the early part of this century, the Supreme Court rigorously applied the Lochner approach and the freedom-of-contract formula derived from it to invalidate statutes regulating the hours of labor, guaranteeing minimum wages, barring so-called yellow-dog contracts (making it a condition of employment that the worker will not join a union), or restraining the granting of injunctions in labor disputes.

Restrictions on Commerce Power. The Court's use of substantive due process to strike down state statutes interfering with freedom of contract in the conduct of business and labor relations was paralleled by its restrictive approach to the commerce clause. In *Gibbons v. Ogden* the Marshall Court had construed the clause in an expansive manner. After Marshall's time, the Court tended to limit the broad Marshall scope. This tendency was not, at first, of great practical importance, for the federal commerce power was rarely exercised during the first part of the nation's history. But the same factors which led the states to seek to intercede in the economic sphere toward the end of the century also induced similar federal activity. The abuses of industrialism increasingly called forth regulatory laws from Washington—starting with the Interstate Commerce Act of 1887, the pioneer regulatory statute based upon the commerce power. It was with the enactment of that law, the high bench has said, "that the interstate commerce power began to exert positive influence on American law and life."

It was at this point, when the federal government felt called upon to intervene actively in economic affairs, that the Supreme Court's tendency to narrow the commerce power became of the greatest consequence. Decisions of the Court withdrew from federal authority a large part of the area of economic activity. A series of decisions held that production or manufacturing was not commerce subject to Congressional authority, even though undertaken with the intent that the products should be transported across state lines. And the same came to be true of mining and agriculture. These, too, were ruled purely local events, not part of the interstate commerce subject to federal control, even where the end result was the shipment of the mineral or farm products to other states.

What this restricted conception of commerce meant in practice was shown by *United States v. E. C. Knight Co.* (1895), which arose out of the first important prosecution under the Sherman Anti-Trust Act of 1890. The defendant company had obtained a virtual monopoly over the manufacture of refined sugar in this country. The complaint charged that the defendant had violated the Sherman Act by its acquisition of its principal competitors, several sugar-refining companies in Pennsylvania. The Supreme Court held, however, that such acquisition could not be reached by the federal commerce power. The monopolistic acts alleged related only to manufacturing, which under the view already stated was not within the scope of the commerce clause.

The effect of the Knight decision was to defeat the main object for which the Sherman Act was passed. It was not, indeed, until the Knight restriction was substantially watered down that the Anti-Trust Law itself could effectively be employed as a weapon against practices in restraint of trade. "The Knight decision," said the Supreme Court in 1948, "made the statute a dead letter . . . and had its full force remained unmodified, the Act today would be a weak instrument."

The Child Labor Case. But the Court went even further, in the first part of this century, in restricting the broad scope which the Marshall Court had given to the federal commerce power. This is strikingly shown by the 1918 Child Labor Case. It involved the constitutionality of a federal statute which prohibited the transportation in interstate commerce of goods made in factories that employed children. Though the statute did not in terms interfere with local production or manufacturing, its real purpose was to suppress child labor. With goods produced by children denied their interstate market, child labor could not continue upon a widespread scale. To the majority of the Court, the Congressional purpose rendered the law invalid. Congress was seeking primarily to regulate the manner in which manufacturing was carried on; such manufacturing, under the restrictive meaning of the Court, was not commerce which could be reached by federal authority. Congress could not, even by an act whose terms were specifically limited to regulation of commerce, use its commerce power to exert authority over matters like manufacturing which were not, within the Court's restricted notion, commerce.

The narrow judicial approach had a particularly distressing result in the Child Labor Case. "If there is any matter," asserted Justice Holmes in dissent, "upon which civilized countries have agreed . . . it is the evil of premature and excessive child labor." Yet the practical result of the decision was to render effective regulation of child labor impossible. If a practice like child labor is to be dealt with effectually, it must be by national regulation. By rigidly excluding Congress from exercising regulatory authority, the Child Labor Case virtually decreed that child labor should be left only to the workings of an unrestrained system of laissez-faire. The United States alone, among nations, was precluded from taking effective action against an evil so widely censured by civilized opinion.

Holmes and Brandeis Dissenting. The restrictive interpretation of governmental authority by the Supreme Court was adopted over increasingly frequent dissents by justices who took a more expansive view of public power. In particular, opposition to the Court majority gave voice to the now-classic dissents of Justices Holmes and Brandeis. Though quite different in their backgrounds and personalities, the two dissenters represented the new jurisprudence that was to challenge and ultimately supplant the view which prevailed on the Court in the post-1890 period. They found themselves in dissent together in most of the important cases applying the restrictive approach already outlined.

The Holmes-Brandeis dissents flatly rejected the notion of the Court as supreme censor of the wisdom of challenged legislation. Such notion meant, in practice, Brandeis once asserted, that "judges have decided a law unconstitutional simply because they considered a law unwise." To the dissenters, the judges had no such right. On the contrary, "their business is not to decide whether the view taken by the legislature is a wise view, but whether a body of men could reasonably hold such a view." As Holmes expressed it in his celebrated Lochner dissent, a statute should not be ruled invalid "unless it can be said that a rational and fair man necessarily would admit that the statute proposed would infringe fundamental principles as they have been understood by the traditions of our people and our law." (*See Reading No. 13.*)

In the Holmes-Brandeis view, the test is whether a reasonable legislator—the Congressional version of the "reasonable man"—could have adopted a law like that at issue. Is the statute as applied so clearly arbitrary or capricious that legislators acting reasonably could not have believed it to be necessary or appropriate for the public welfare?

To Holmes and Brandeis, the approach in decisions like *Lochner v. New York* and the Child Labor Case was particularly objectionable because it virtually elevated the laissez-faire doctrine to the constitutional plane. The judges, Brandeis declared, were "largely deaf and blind" to economic and social needs: "They applied complacently eighteenth century conceptions of the liberty of the individual and of the sacredness of private property. Early nineteenth century scientific half-truths, like 'The survival of the fittest,' which translated into practice meant 'The devil take the hindmost,' were erected by judicial sanction into a moral law."

The Constitution, stated Holmes in a noted passage, "is not intended to embody a particular economic theory, whether of paternalism and the organic relation of the citizen to the state or of laissez faire." But it was most difficult for judges not to assume that the basic document was intended to embody the dominant economic beliefs of their own day. The Constitution, to cite another famous Holmes statement, may not enact Herbert Spencer's *Social Statics*. But the Supreme Court's narrow notion of governmental power was a necessary complement to the translation of Spencerian economics into American constitutional law.

CHAPTER 8

The New Deal and "Court-Packing"

New Deal Cases. In 1933 the Administration of Franklin D. Roosevelt took office. Its program sought to resuscitate the depressed economy by extended federal intervention. The New Deal involved the very negation of laissez-faire, and it meant a degree of governmental control from Washington far greater than any previously attempted. If the country was to go forward, said President Roosevelt in his inaugural address in 1932, "we must move as a trained and loyal army willing to sacrifice for the good of a common discipline, because without such discipline no progress is made, no leadership becomes effective."

The effort to move the nation forward, however, came up against the restricted view of the commerce power which had been developed by the Supreme Court. The result was a series of decisions which struck down most of the important New Deal legislation. In 1935 and 1936 cases, the Court ruled invalid the two most important antidepression measures of the New Deal—the National Industrial Recovery Act and the Agricultural Adjustment Act. The NIRA was held beyond the reach of Congressional power as applied to small wholesale poultry dealers in Brooklyn. The business done by them was ruled purely local in character, even though the poultry handled by them came from outside the state. And, under the Court's approach, it made no difference that there was some effect upon interstate commerce by the business being regulated. Similarly, in holding the AAA unconstitutional, the Court relied upon the proposition that agriculture, like manufacturing or mining, is not commerce and hence is immune from federal control. In another 1936 case, the same approach was applied to a federal law regulating the bituminous coal industry by price-fixing, proscription of unfair trade practices, and prescription of labor conditions.

The restrictive interpretation of the commerce power in these New Deal decisions was catastrophic in its consequences upon effective regulation. Elimination of manufacturing, mining, agriculture, and other productive industries from the reach of the commerce clause rendered Congress powerless to deal with problems in those fields, however pressing they might become. And so, as Justice Jackson stated, "a national government that has power, through the Federal Trade Commission, to prohibit the giving of prizes with penny candy shipped by the manufacturer from one state to another, was powerless to deal with the causes of critical stoppages in the gigantic bituminous coal industry."

This comment drew special pertinence from the grim economic background behind the New Deal measures. Giant industries prostrate, crises in production and consumption throughout the country, the economy in a state of virtual collapse—if ever there was a need for exertion of federal power, it was after the collapse of 1929. If federal power was not to be as broad as that need, it meant that the nation was helpless in the face of economic disaster.

Court-Packing Plan. According to President Roosevelt, the Court's decisions "stopped short" the New Deal program and tipped the governmental balance of power completely out of balance. By his "Court-packing" plan of February 5, 1937, F.D.R. sought to restore the balance. The President's message did not, however, refer to the need to change the high bench's course of decision. Instead, it was cast in terms of the need to remedy the justices' inability to carry their heavy burden because of the infirmities of age and the need for "constant infusion of new blood." F.D.R. asked for authority to appoint a new justice where an incumbent justice reached the retirement age of seventy and failed to retire. The proposal could have given the President the authority to appoint as many as six new justices. (*See Reading No. 14.*)

F.D.R.'s plan generated bitter opposition which found a responsive chord in the nation's instinctive need of an independent constitutional arbiter. In part this was true because of the overartful attempt to conceal the true nature of the attack on the Court. The President purported only to deal with the problem of an overage judiciary unable to cope with an overcrowded docket. But age itself was palpably not the difficulty: the examples of Brandeis and Hughes on the 1936 Court (not to mention that of Holmes a few years earlier) showed that clearly. Nor was the Court behind in its work; in fact, under Chief Justice Hughes the work schedule was probably managed better than at any other time in its history. (*See Reading No. 15.*)

That the Court-packing plan failed, though sponsored by one of our most popular Presidents in the prime of his power, is the best testimonial to the position and prestige attained by the Supreme Court among the American people. After lengthy hearings and public discussion, F.D.R.'s plan was rejected by the Senate Judiciary Committee. Only relatively minor provisions were contained in the watered-down Judiciary Act of 1937, and none of them affected the personnel or powers of the Supreme Court.

Constitutional Revolution. If President Roosevelt had thus lost the Court-packing battle, he was, nevertheless, ultimately to win the constitutional war, for the Supreme Court itself was soon to abandon its restrictive approach to the proper scope of governmental power. Hence, in Justice Jackson's summary of the Court-packing fight, "Each side of the controversy has comforted itself with a claim of victory. The President's enemies defeated the court reform bill—the President achieved court reform."

Early in 1937 there took place a remarkable reversal in the Supreme Court's attitude toward the New Deal program. Before that time (1934-1936), the Court rendered twelve decisions declaring invalid legislative measures of the New Deal; starting in April 1937 that tribunal upheld every New Deal law presented to it, including some that were basically similar to earlier statutes which it had nullified. It is, in truth, not too far-fetched to assert that in 1937 there took place a veritable revolution in the Court's jurisprudence, which Edward S. Corwin has appropriately characterized as "Constitutional Revolution, Ltd."

It is too facile to state that the 1937 change was only a protective response to the Court-packing plan—to assert, as did so many contemporary wags, that "a switch in time saved Nine." It would be idle to deny that the furor over the President's proposal did have repercussions within the Court's marble halls. As F.D.R. himself expressed it, "It would be a little naive to refuse to recognize some connection between these 1937 decisions and the Supreme Court fight." At the same time, it misconceives the nature of the Supreme Court and its manner of operation as a judicial tribunal to assume that the 1937 change in jurisprudence was solely the result of the Court-packing plan. The 1937 reversal reflected changes in legal ideology common to the entire legal profession. The extreme individualistic philosophy upon which the justices had been nurtured has been shaken to its foundations during the present century. If Spencerian laissez-faire gave way on the bench to the judicial pragmatism of Justice Holmes, it was only because a similar movement had taken place in the country as a whole.

At any rate, there is little doubt that there was a real conversion in a majority of the Supreme Court and that its effects do justify the "constitutional revolution" characterization. It is usually overlooked that the decisions first signaling the reversal in jurisprudence were reached before the President had even announced his Court-packing plan. On March 29, 1937, Chief Justice Hughes announced a decision upholding a state minimum wage law, basically similar to one which the Court had held to be beyond the power of both states and nation to enact only nine months previously. But, though the Court's confession of error was announced a month after the President's proposal, the case itself was decided in conference among the justices about a month before the Court-packing plan was announced. The circumstantial evidence available to us on this point strongly bears out the statement made some years later by Chief Justice Hughes to his authorized biographer: "The President's proposal had not the slightest effect on our decision."

The Jones & Laughlin Case. In April 1937 the Court decided *National Labor Relations Board v. Jones & Laughlin Steel Corp.* and upheld the constitutionality of the National Labor Relations Act. That 1935 law was the Magna Carta of the American labor movement; it guaranteed the right of employees to organize collectively and made it an unfair labor practice for employers to interfere with such right. The Act was intended to apply to industries throughout the nation, to those engaged in production and manufacture as well as to those engaged in commerce, literally speaking. But this appeared to bring it directly in conflict with the Supreme Court decisions drastically limiting the scope of federal authority over interstate commerce, including some of the 1934-1936 period on which the ink was scarcely dry.

In Jones & Laughlin, these precedents were not followed: "These cases," laconically stated the Court, "are not controlling here." Instead, the opinion gave the federal power over interstate commerce its maximum sweep. Mines, mills, and factories, whose activities had formerly been ruled "local," and hence immune from federal regulation, were now held to affect interstate commerce directly enough to justify Congressional control. There is little doubt that, as the dissenting justices protested, Congress in the Labor Relations Act exercised a power of control over purely local industry beyond anything theretofore deemed permissible. In truth, as the dissenters accurately stated, in characterizing the effect of the Court's reinterpretation of the commerce power, "Almost anything—marriage, birth, death—may in some fashion affect commerce."

Darby and Other Cases. Jones & Laughlin marks a definite break with the pre-1937 Court's imposition of restrictions upon the commerce power; under it, as pointed out, manufacturing as such is not automatically excluded from the reach of the federal authority. Later cases extend the Jones & Laughlin approach to mining and agriculture. In 1940 the Court upheld a new Congressional act regulating the bituminous coal industry, similar in many ways to that which had been annulled in 1936. Similarly, in 1939 the Court held valid the Agricultural Adjustment Act of 1938, whose basic features were not unlike those of the law of the same name condemned in 1936.

Jones & Laughlin and the later cases referred to are based upon the conception that the Congressional power to *regulate* under the commerce clause is a complete one. That power, said the Jones & Laughlin opinion, is plenary and may be exerted to foster, protect, control, and restrain commerce. That being the case, there has been no room in the post-1937 Court for a decision like that in the Child Labor Case (discussed in Chapter 7), which invalidated an admitted regulation of interstate commerce because the Congressional purpose had been to regulate indirectly local economic activities which were beyond the reach of the commerce power.

After decisions in 1938 and 1939 eroding the constitutional basis of the Child Labor Case, the Court in 1941 expressly overruled that case. This occurred in *United States v. Darby*, where the legality of the Fair Labor Standards Act of 1938 was at issue. That law provided for the fixing of minimum wages and maximum hours. It prohibited the shipment in interstate commerce of goods manufactured by employees whose wages are less than the prescribed minimum or whose hours of work are more than the prescribed maximum. As such, it was not unlike the law at issue in the Child Labor Case, which had prohibited the transportation in interstate commerce of goods produced by child labor. In its Darby decision, nonetheless, the Court refused to follow the reasoning of the Child Labor Case. Under Darby, the end toward which a Congressional exercise of regulatory power is directed is irrelevant. Darby definitely disowned the Child Labor Case thesis that the motive of the prohibition could operate to deprive the Congressional regulation of its constitutional validity. Instead the Court relied directly upon the Marshall definition of the power to regulate commerce as the power "to prescribe the rule by which commerce is governed." "Whatever their motive and purpose," declared the Darby opinion, "regulations of commerce which do not infringe some constitutional prohibition are within the plenary power conferred on Congress by the Commerce Clause." Thus had the wheel of constitutional construction swung full circle in the century after Marshall's death.

CHAPTER 9

Judicial Restraint, War, and Cold War

Due Process Decline. The decisions since 1937 signal a significant change in the Supreme Court's role in the constitutional structure. Where the Court had previously set itself up as virtual supreme censor of the wisdom of challenged legislation, it has since adopted the view formerly expressed in dissent by Justice Holmes. Under the earlier approach, the desirability of a statute as determined as an objective fact on the Court's own independent judgment. Today a more subjective test is applied: could rational legislators have regarded the statute as a reasonable method of reaching the desired result?

The change in the Court's approach has had tremendous impact upon the doctrine of substantive due process. Few today doubt that the high tribunal went too far before 1937 in its application of the doctrine or that the Court since that time has been correct in deliberately discarding the extreme due process philosophy. The due process clause was not intended to prevent legislatures from choosing whether to regulate or leave their economies to the blind operation of uncontrolled economic forces, futile or even noxious though the choice might seem to the judge. Economic views of confined validity are not be treated as though the Framers had enshrined them in the Constitution.

In his dissent in the Lochner case, as noted earlier, Justice Holmes asserted, "This case is decided upon an economic theory which a large part of the country does not entertain." In the period since 1937 both the economic and legal theories upon which Lochner rested have been repudiated by the Supreme Court. Early in 1937 the high tribunal overruled its earlier holdings that a minimum-wage law violated due process by impairing freedom of contract between employers and employees. "What is this freedom?" asked the Court's opinion. "The Constitution does not speak of freedom of contract." The liberty safeguarded by the Constitution is liberty in a society which requires the protection of law against evils which menace the health, safety, morals, or welfare of the people. Regulation adopted in the interests of the community, the Court concluded, is due process.

Since 1937 the high bench has had occasion directly to overrule only one other due-process decision of its predecessors. This occurred in 1941, when a 1928 decision voiding as inconsistent with due process a state statute regulating the fees charged by employment agencies had been relied on by a lower court to invalidate a similar Nebraska law; the Supreme Court speedily reversed, holding that the earlier case could no longer be deemed controlling authority.

Though the Court has had no occasion directly to repudiate other specific due-process decisions of the pre-1937 period, there is no doubt that it would do so if the need arose, for recent decisions show how clearly the Court has rejected the earlier due process philosophy. From 1890 to 1937 the high bench used the due process clause as a device to enable it to review the desirability of regulatory legislation. In 1955 the Court could declare, "The day is gone when this Court uses the Due Process Clause of the Fourteenth Amendment to strike down state laws, regulatory of business and industrial conditions, because they may be unwise, improvident, or out of harmony with a particular school of thought."

During the past thirty years no regulatory law has been invalidated by the Supreme Court on due process grounds. The view that due process authorizes courts to hold laws unconstitutional because they believe the legislature has acted unwisely has definitely been discarded. As the Court put it in 1963, "We have returned to the original constitutional proposition that courts do not substitute their social and economic beliefs for the judgment of legislative bodies, who are elected to pass laws." Above all, it is not for the Court to judge the correctness of the economic theory behind a regulatory law. Not only has the Holmes view that the Constitution does not enact Spencer's *Social Statics* been emphatically adopted; in the Court's recent words, "Whether the legislature takes for its textbook Adam Smith, Herbert Spencer, Lord Keynes, or some other is no concern of ours."

The decline of substantive due process is now firmly ingrained in the jurisprudence of the highest bench. And, that tribunal would say, such rejection is entirely consistent with the role of the judiciary in a representative democracy. To draw the pre-1937 due process line as a limit to regulatory action is to make the criterion of constitutionality what the judges believe to be correct as a matter of economic theory.

The Second World War. The change from judicial supremacy to the judicial restraint of the post-1937 period gained added emphasis during World War II and the postwar tension which followed that conflict. During the second global conflict, as during the Civil War period, the Supreme Court did little more than confirm the action taken by the government to deal with the war emergency. Executive primacy is an inevitable concomitant of full-scale war, and it is perhaps unfair to expect the justices to do more than stamp with their imprimatur measures deemed necessary by those wielding the force of the nation. Certainly the Court could do no more than ratify the plenary power vested in government to meet the needs of global war. The power fully to mobilize manpower had been recognized by the Court during World War I; hence, as the Court put it in 1948, "The constitutionality of the conscription of manpower for military service is beyond question." The decisions arising out of World War II recognized in the government authority over property rights as extensive as that possessed by it over manpower. Said the Court, in the case just quoted from, with regard to the impact of "total global warfare" upon our system: "With the advent of such warfare, mobilized property in the form of equipment and supplies became as essential as mobilized manpower. Mobilization of effort extended not only to the uniformed armed services but to the entire population. . . . The language of the Constitution authorizing such measures is broad rather than restrictive."

In many ways the most dramatic of the Court's war decisions was rendered in the case of the eight German saboteurs who had been landed on our shores from submarines in June 1942. The eight had been arrested by FBI agents soon after their landings and tried by a military commission specially appointed by President Roosevelt for offenses against the law of war and the Articles of War. The commission had found them guilty of violating the law of war by attempting sabotage of our war facilities and had ordered death sentences for six of them and prison terms for the other two. The officers who had been appointed to defend the saboteurs before the military tribunal then sought habeas corpus. To deal with the cases "without any avoidable delay," after the lower courts had refused relief, the Supreme Court convened in June 1942, in special term. After hearing argument for two days, it handed down a brief *per curiam* opinion denying habeas corpus. A formal opinion by Chief Justice Stone, setting forth the reasoning of the Court, was not filed until three months later—weeks after the death sentences ordered by the military commission had been carried out.

Before the Supreme Court, the German saboteurs had contended that they could not validly be tried by a military tribunal, asserting that they were entitled to be tried in the civil courts with the safeguards, including trial by jury, which the Fifth and Sixth Amendments guarantee to all persons tried in such courts for criminal offenses. The Court rejected their contention, holding that the constitutional safeguards did not apply to offenses against the law of war.

Japanese Evacuation. Few, it is believed, will take issue with the Court's decision in the case of the German saboteurs. But the same is scarcely true of the high bench's handling of what a *Harper's* article was to term "America's Greatest Wartime Mistake," namely, the evacuation of those of Japanese ancestry from the West Coast.

Acting upon their belief that those of Japanese blood posed a security threat after Pearl Harbor, the military moved to eliminate the danger by a number of restrictive measures. The most important of them were a series of Civilian Exclusion Orders, issued early in 1942, excluding "all persons of Japanese ancestry, both alien and non-alien," from the westernmost part of the country. Those so excluded were gathered together in so-called assembly centers and then evacuated to what were euphemistically termed relocation centers in interior states, where they were detained until almost the end of the war. Under this evacuation program, over 112,000 persons of Japanese ancestry were herded from their homes on the West Coast into the relocation centers, which, had they been set up in any other country, we would not hesitate to call by their true name of concentration camps.

The record of this government in dealing with the West Coast Japanese during the war is hardly one which an American can contemplate with satisfaction. As the high Court eloquently declared in 1943, "Distinctions between citizens solely because of their ancestry are by their very nature odious to a free people whose institutions are founded upon the doctrine of equality." Despite this, the Court did uphold the evacuation of the Japanese (though with three strong dissents) in *Korematsu v. United States* (1944). Korematsu had been convicted for remaining in a military area contrary to the Civilian Exclusion Order of the military commander. Such an order, said the Court, could validly be issued by the military authorities in the light of the particular situation confronting them on the West Coast after Pearl Harbor. In the face of a threatened Japanese attack, citizens of Japanese ancestry could rationally be set apart from those who had no particular associations with Japan; in time of war residents having ethnic affiliations with an invading enemy may be a greater source of danger than those of a different ancestry. That being the case, it could not be said that the exclusion order bore no reasonable relation to the demands of military necessity. It was not until December 1944 that the Court ordered the release of the Japanese-Americans from the relocation centers, on the ground that, though the original evacuations might have been justified by necessity, such necessity did not exist three years after Pearl Harbor, during which time the government had had ample opportunity to separate the loyal from the disloyal among those detained.

The Cold War. The postwar decade of international tension had important effects in Supreme Court jurisprudence. The excesses of the cold war period found their echo in decisions rendered under the influence of the post-1937 doctrine of judicial restraint. We are perhaps too close to some of the excesses committed during the postwar period to be able to write impartially of it. These excesses did, however, teach us that security, like the patriotism of which Dr. Johnson speaks, might also come to be the last refuge of a scoundrel; many were the things done in security's name in a time of tension that would not be tolerated at other times.

A basic problem for the Supreme Court in a system like ours is that of reconciling the antinomy between liberty and security. Both have, to be sure, always been essential elements in the polity, whose coexistence has had to be reconciled by the law. In the cold war period, nevertheless, it was the element of security that tended to dominate. The response of our government to the tensions of the cold war made our law security-conscious as it had never before been in our history.

The governmental demand for security was articulated in important laws and other measures restricting rights normally deemed fundamental. For the first time since the notorious Alien and Sedition Acts of 1798 themselves, a peacetime sedition law (making subversive speech alone criminal) was used to put people in prison. The law in question—the Smith Act—was enacted in 1940; but the first significant prosecutions, those brought in 1948 against the leaders of the American Communist Party, were a direct fruit of the postwar confrontation between the West and the Soviet Union. The Communist prosecutions were upheld by the Supreme Court in *Dennis v. United States* (1951), with the decision turning on the "clear and present danger" presented by Communist advocacy during the tensions of the postwar period.

In addition, the Court upheld other significant cold war restrictions, ranging from drastic restraints upon aliens to the loyalty-security programs instituted by governments in this country. The restrictions on Communist aliens were ruled within the plenary power of Congress over citizens of other lands, and the federal loyalty program was upheld under the "settled principle that government employment . . . can be revoked at the will of the appointing officer." In addition, the Court refused to strike down restrictions upon the procedural rights of notice and full hearing in cases where national security was involved.

The decisions referred to, which occurred during the immediate postwar period, may be understandable as a continued reaction from the excesses of pre-1937 judicial supremacy. Justices who had repudiated those excesses continued to display the same Holmesian approach of deference to the legislator. One may wonder, nevertheless, whether the high bench did not go too far in standing aside in the face of the extreme restrictions imposed in security's name. A Court overimbued with the dominant demand for security may tend to give effect to that demand, even if the cost be distortion of accepted principles of constitutional law. Yet this can hardly be done without important effects upon general jurisprudence. A tribunal that molds its law only to fit the immediate demands of public sentiment is hardly fulfilling the role proper to the supreme bench in a system such as ours. As Justice Frankfurter once put it, "The Court has no reason for existence if it merely reflects the pressures of the day." The doctrine of deference to the legislature may require abnegation on the part of the Court but hardly abdication by it of the judicial function. Certainly, whatever may be said about the strains and stresses of the cold war period, the enemy was not so near the gates that we had to abandon respect for the organic traditions that had theretofore prevailed in our system.

CHAPTER 10

The Warren Court

Warren and the Court. John Adams as President is remembered, as much as anything else, for his appointment of Marshall as Chief Justice. The same may well be true of Dwight Eisenhower and his selection of Earl Warren to head the Supreme Court. From 1953 to the present, Warren has placed the impress of his strong personality upon the high bench. It is as the Warren Court that the present tribunal will be known to legal historians. It will bear the hallmark of Earl Warren as unmistakably as prior courts bore those of his predecessors.

One who looks only to the bare legal powers of the Chief Justice may find it hard to understand this underscoring of his preeminence. Aside from his designation as chief of the Court and the attribution to him of a slightly higher salary, his position is not legally superior to that of his colleagues. In Justice Clark's recent words, "the Chief Justice has no more authority than other members of the court." (*See Reading No. 20.*)

This approach to the Chief Justiceship, while true in a formalistic sense, overlooks the extralegal potential inherent in that position. The Chief Justice may be only *primus inter pares;* but he is clearly *primus.* Somebody has to preside over a body of nine men, and it is the chief who does preside, both in open court and in the even more important work of deciding cases in the conference chamber. It is the Chief Justice who directs the business of the Court. He controls the discussion in conference; his is the prerogative to call and discuss cases before the other justices speak. In this respect his role has been well said to be that of striking the pitch, as it were, for the orchestra. It is his example that will, most often, set the tone of the entire conference session.

In addition, it has become settled by custom that it is for the Chief Justice to assign the writing of opinions. This function has been called the most important that pertains to the office of chief. In discharging it, a great Chief Justice has been likened to a general deploying his army. It is he who determines what use will be made of the Court's personnel; his employment of the assigning power will influence both the growth of the law and his own relations with his colleagues.

Charles Evans Hughes' manner of presiding over the Court was once compared to Toscanini's manner of leading an orchestra. If the exact same claim cannot be made for Warren's leadership, still it cannot be denied that he has brought more authority to the Chief Justiceship than it has had since Hughes. Before Warren the dominant theme on the high bench was discord; all too often the Court presented a far from edifying spectacle of internal atomization. To be sure, judicial dissension did not turn into sweetness and light merely because of Warren's appointment to the central chair. Sharp divisions have existed on the Warren bench. But these differences are no longer, as they all too often were before, reflections of personal antagonisms. Intellectual issues have once again come to be dealt with purely as such. Under Warren, for almost the first time since Hughes' retirement, dissonance ceased to be a major Court characteristic.

The restoration of its institutional ethos to a Court that was sorely in need of it has, indeed, been Earl Warren's primary contribution. And it is one which outranks any that he has been able to make to our substantive law. It may be, as John Winthrop said in 1644, that "Judges are Gods upon earth." But a pantheon that speaks with nine inconsistent voices can hardly inspire the listener with the feeling of divine certainty.

It is a mistake to conceive of the Chief Justiceship solely in terms of learning in the law. Of course the Supreme Court is a law court, but it is, and has been since Marshall, unique among courts. Public, not private law is the stuff of its litigation. Elevation to it requires adjustment from preoccupation with the restricted, however novel, problems of private litigation to the most exacting demands of judicial statesmanship. On such a tribunal the judge must be even more the statesman than the lawyer.

This is particularly true of the man who sits at the center of the Court. The main monument of Warren's judicial statesmanship is, without a doubt, the 1954 decision in the School

Segregation Case. It was under Warren's lead that the Court seized the vital constitutional issue by the bit (the same issue which had been meticulously avoided under Warren's predecessor) and unanimously outlawed school segregation. The element of unanimity cannot be overemphasized. It was no mean feat for the Court's neophyte (as he then was), vested only with the moral prestige of the Chief Justiceship, to induce eight individualists, accustomed to arriving at decisions in their own ways and never hesitant at articulating their separate views, to join in the unanimous decision—without even a single concurring voice to detract from the majesty and forthrightness of his opinion.

Though Warren's chief contribution to the Court has been on the administrative side, his influence on the substantive law dispensed by the high tribunal should not be overlooked. In this respect, Warren's approach has differed drastically from that of his predecessor. In cases involving conflicts between government and the individual, Chief Justice Vinson was usually on the side of officialdom. Warren, on the other hand, has started with a strong predisposition in favor of the individual. It has been under Warren's leadership that the Vinson Court, almost invariably on the side of governmental authority, has been replaced by a tribunal inclined to look on claims of violation of individual right with a far more friendly eye. "When the generation of 1980 receives from us the Bill of Rights," Warren has said, "the document will not have exactly the same meaning it had when we received it from our fathers." The Bill of Rights as it has been interpreted by the Warren Court already has a meaning much different from that handed down to it by its predecessor.

Emphasis on Personal Rights. The Warren Court's focus upon the Bill of Rights has led to increasing emphasis in its decisions upon personal rights. Thus there has been a significant shift in the present Court, as compared with its predecessors, from the protection of property to protection of the person. If, in 1922, a federal judge could assert "that of the three fundamental principles which underlie government, and for which government exists, the protection of life, liberty, and property, the chief of these is property," the judicial emphasis in our own day has surely shifted in favor of the other two. While most of the work of the pre-1937 Supreme Court had concerned the protection of *property* rights against what were conceived as governmental violations of due process, in the Warren Court the judicial concern has focused upon *personal* rights. It may, indeed, be said that the primary role played by the high bench today is as guardian of civil liberties.

In 1886 as discerning an observer as Sir Henry Maine could refer to our Bill of Rights as "a certain number of amendments on comparatively unimportant points." Today such an observation could scarcely be made by anyone the least conversant with American constitutional law. On the contrary, the Bill of Rights and the Fourteenth Amendment, making its basic safeguards binding upon the states as well, have become the very stuff of which our constitutional law is now made.

In enforcing the civil liberties guaranteed by the basic document, the Supreme Court has forged for itself a new and vital place in the constitutional structure. More and more the high tribunal has come to display its solicitude for the personal rights of the individual. Freedom of speech, press, religion, the rights of minorities and those accused of crime, those of individuals subjected to legislative and administrative inquisitions —all have, in recent years, come under the Court's fostering guardianship.

Racial Equality. Perhaps the most important work done by the Supreme Court in the field of civil liberties has been its protection of the rights of minorities. "The most certain test." says Lord Acton, "by which we judge whether a country is really free is the amount of security enjoyed by minorities." From this point of view, the situation in much of the United States not too long ago was far from encouraging. Despite the intent of their framers, the post-Civil War amendments were all but read out of the Constitution, so far as ameliorating the legal position of the Negro was concerned.

It is only recently that the changed attitude of the Supreme Court to the protection of personal rights has made equal protection and due process more than mere slogans for minority groups. Particularly with regard to racial discriminations, there has been a complete alteration in the judicial attitude. For virtually the first time since their adoption, the gulf between the letter of the Fourteenth and Fifteenth Amendments and their practical effect has been significantly narrowed. In its decisions the Supreme Court has removed the legal prop from the most important manifestations of racial discrimination in this country. In an important 1944 case, the so-called white primary, upon which Southern efforts to disfranchise the Negro were based, was ruled unconstitutional. In 1948 the enforcement of racial restrictive covenants was stricken down.

It has, however, been in the Warren Court that the most significant decisions have been rendered. In the landmark 1954 case of *Brown v. Board of Education,* the enforced segregation upon which the whole pattern of Southern discrimination against the Negro has depended was held violative of the equal protection clause. The Brown decision outlawing segregation in schools was as momentous as any ever rendered by a judicial tribunal, for make no mistake about it, it will ultimately have an impact upon a whole community's way of life comparable to that caused by the most drastic political revolution or military conflict.

The road to the Brown decision was pointed to by the proviso of equality laid down in the 1896 case of *Plessy v. Ferguson,* whose "separate but equal" doctrine had been the legal cornerstone of Southern segregation. Starting in 1937 the Supreme Court began to emphasize the requirement of equality in the separate facilities provided for the Negro in the field of education. The cases from 1937 to 1954 placed ever-increasing stress upon the judicial implementation of the requirement of equality in facilities. The Court's decisions tended toward the doctrine that, where higher education is concerned, separate facilities for the Negro are inherently unequal. From there it was a short, though vital, step to the Brown decision itself, for what is true of segregation in higher education is also true of segregation as such. There can never be real equality in separated facilities, for the mere fact of segregation makes for discrimination. The arbitrary separation of the Negro, solely on the basis of race, is, in the phrase of the Plessy dissent, a "badge of servitude" and must generate in him a feeling of inferior social status, regardless of the formal equality of the facilities provided for him. And if that be the case, then, as the Brown decision ruled, segregation as such is discriminatory and hence a denial of the equal protection of the laws demanded by the Constitution.

Interposition. As is well known, implementation of the Brown decision has seen the revival in our own day of controversy between state and federal power. The ghost of state sovereignty, which (one would have thought) had been laid to rest by Appomattox, has suddenly stirred from its deserved repose.

Shortly after the Supreme Court announced its decisions holding the segregation of Negroes in schools unconstitutional, so-called resolutions of "interposition" were adopted by the legislatures of several Southern states. That passed in Georgia in 1956 is typical of all of them and may be referred to for illustrative purposes. Expressly labeled a resolution "to invoke the doctrine of interposition," it asserts that the Brown decision and cases following its doctrine are "null, void and of no force or effect." In view of this, the resolution goes on, the state declares its firm intention to take all appropriate measures against this "illegal encroachment upon the rights of her people." (*See Reading No. 17.*)

As a matter of constitutional law, such state assertions of a right of interposition are no more valid than those stricken down so decisively in Marshall's and Taney's day. In the 1958 case of *Cooper v. Aaron,* the Supreme Court was presented directly with the claim that the Governor and legislature of Arkansas were not bound by the decision invalidating school segregation. This contention was disposed of in incisive terms. No principle, said the Court, is more firmly established in American public law than that binding the states to interpretations by the highest tribunal of the supreme law of the land. *Marbury v. Madison* "declared the basic principle that the federal judiciary is supreme in the exposition of the law of the Constitution, and that principle has ever since been respected by this Court and the Country as a permanent and indispensable feature of our constitutional system." The conclusion is consequently clear that interposition is not a *constitutional* doctrine. At best it is illegal defiance of constitutional authority. If the states can nullify federal action in the manner claimed by advocates of the interposition doctrine, the Constitution itself, declares the *Cooper v.*

Aaron opinion (repeating a famous statement of Marshall), "becomes a solemn mockery." (*See Reading No. 18.*)

From a strictly legal point of view, perhaps, *Cooper v. Aaron* may appear to constitute merely the superfluous hammering of nails into the coffin of dead constitutional doctrine. It is, nevertheless, essential that the law seize every opportunity to repudiate a doctrine so completely opposed to the fundamentals of the American constitutional system. To deny the authority of the highest Court in constitutional questions concerning the states is, in effect, to deny to American federalism the means of operating effectively. In Justice Frankfurter's words, for the states "to use political power to try to paralyze the supreme law, precludes the maintenance of our federal system as we have known and cherished it for one hundred and seventy years."

Federal Arbiter. The controversy over *Brown v. Board of Education* and its progeny and the judicial role in *Cooper v. Aaron* (in maintaining the Constitution as the supreme law of the land) illustrates a second essential part played by the Supreme Court in the present period of our constitutional development—that of arbiter of the federal system. Such role compares in importance with that of the Court as guardian of civil liberties. If federalism is to work, an independent judicial tribunal must be its arbiter. In our system the role of arbiter is performed by the Supreme Court—in cases ranging from those involving state burdens upon interstate commerce to those arising from state infringements upon federal supremacy. In this respect the high bench is the bolt that holds the federal machinery together. Draw it out and there would be no real federal system, only a moral union between the states.

The cases involving exercise of the Court's function of striking a balance between national and state authority that have arisen before the present Court have most frequently involved claimed interferences by the states with interstate commerce. The work of the Court here has insured that national commerce will continue free from crippling state interference. Thus the Court in 1959 invalidated an Illinois law that required all trucks to have a contour type of rear fender mudguard on highways of the state. The law made the conventional or straight mudguard, legal in other states, illegal in Illinois and imposed a substantial financial expense on truckers. Hence, the Court held, the statute resulted in a "rather massive . . . burden on interstate commerce."

Criminal Justice. No concern has been closer to the Warren Court than that of ensuring fair play and equality in the field of criminal justice. And no Court in American history has given more effect to such concern in its jurisprudence. It is not too much, indeed, to say that the decisions of the Warren Court have worked a complete change in the criminal law and its application by policemen, prosecutors, and judges.

In the first place, the Court under Warren has applied the concept of equality in the criminal field more broadly than any of its predecessors had done. The landmark case here has been *Griffin v. Illinois* (1965), where the Court held that it violates the Fourteenth Amendment for a state to deny to defendants alleging poverty free transcripts of the trial proceedings which would enable them adequately to prosecute appeals from criminal convictions. The state law at issue in Griffin conditioning appeal on the purchase of a transcript applied on its face to rich and poor alike. Its effect, however, was to deny an appeal to potential appellants lacking sufficient funds to purchase a transcript. The Court, laying to rest the notion that equal protection requires only equal laws and that the state is never obliged to equalize economic disparities, held the law unconstitutional. According to the Court, "There can be no equal justice where the kind of trial a man gets depends on the amount of money he has. Destitute defendants must be afforded as adequate appellate review as defendants who have money enough to buy transcripts." (*See Reading No. 16.*)

The Griffin decision has been important both in other decisions extending equality in the criminal field and as a stimulus in focusing concern throughout the land on moving beyond formal equality before the law to the taking of practical steps to ensure that rich and poor are treated as equally as possible before the bar of justice. In addition, it is the Griffin approach that was really the foundation of the now-famous 1963 decision in *Gideon v. Wainwright,* which ruled that the Constitution requires indigent criminal defendants, upon their request, to be furnished court-appointed counsel—a holding which later cases have extended to virtually every stage of the criminal process, from arrest to appeal. Under Gideon and its progeny, no man may be condemned because of poverty to run the gantlet of the criminal law without counsel at his side. Any other practice is so repugnant to the fundamentals of fair play that it may not be squared with due process.

The right to counsel, made effective by the Gideon decision, has itself served as the basis for the recent restrictions imposed by the Court upon police interrogation and the use of confessions. Under *Escobedo v. Illinois* (1964) and *Miranda v. Arizona* (1966), the right to counsel attaches as soon as an individual is the subject of custodial interrogation by the police. For the police to be able to use any confession, they must show that they gave full warning to the defendant that he had a right to remain silent and to the presence of an attorney, either retained or appointed. With the right to counsel and that to remain silent at the interrogation stage rendered effective, it may be expected that the coercive tactics that have at times characterized police investigative work will soon become a thing of the past.

Reapportionment Cases. In their practical impact upon the society, perhaps the most significant decisions rendered by the Warren Court have been those in the field of legislative reapportionment. Of course many of the Court's recent decisions—particularly those involving desegregation—have been criticized as primarily political in nature. Such criticism, however, ignores the essential nature of the highest bench in our constitutional system. Even those to whom the law is the most esoteric of mysteries should by now know that the Supreme Court makes decisions that are political as much as legal. We have endowed a judicial tribunal with the authority to decide disputes that, in other systems, are fought out at the political level.

In political effect, few decisions of the highest Court have had as great consequence as that rendered in the 1962 case of *Baker v. Carr*. The Court there held that it was within the competence of the federal courts to entertain an action challenging a statute apportioning legislative districts as contrary to the equal protection clause. The result of *Baker v. Carr* is that the remedy for unfairness in districting is in the federal courts, as well as in the legislature itself.

It has become all but constitutional cliché that *Baker v. Carr* has worked a virtual revolution in legislative representation throughout the land. Certainly few decisions in the history of the high Court have had as great an impact as the holding that it was within the judicial jurisdiction to entertain an action challenging voter apportionments as violative of the equal protection clause. The net effect of *Baker v. Carr* and the cases decided under its principle has been to bring about a dramatic change in the manner in which legislative districts are apportioned in this country.

That has been true because, in *Reynolds v. Sims* (1964), the Court ruled that the equal protection clause lays down an "equal population" principle for legislative apportionment. The Constitution, under *Reynolds v. Sims,* demands that legislative districts be apportioned on the basis of substantial equality of population. Where that basis is disregarded, the result is an invalid debasement of the right to vote: "The fact that an individual lives here or there is not a legitimate reason for overweighting or diluting the efficacy of his vote." Instead, the Constitution demands nothing less than substantially equal state legislative representation for all citizens. (*See Reading No. 19.*)

In the short time since the Reapportionment Cases were decided, their doctrine has already worked a drastic alteration in the American political structure. The ultimate outcome is bound to be elimination of much of the disproportionate influence which rural areas have had in choosing legislative personnel and a shifting of the legislative balance to those urban concentrations in which the bulk of Americans now live. Court-ordered reapportionment is more and more giving urban and suburban areas a larger voice in state legislatures, and will do so eventually in Congress.

In the perspective of history the Reapportionment Cases will stand as the natural culmination of the historical development of the right of suffrage. As Chief Justice Warren points out in *Reynolds v. Sims,* "history has seen a continuing expansion of the scope of the right of suffrage in this country." Such expansion has been the American counterpart of the movement for universal suffrage throughout the world, starting with the long struggle which ultimately saw the success of the English electoral-reform movement. The basic principles behind the movements for universal suffrage and electoral reform were those which underlie the high court decisions in the *Baker v. Carr* and *Reynolds v. Sims* line of cases. Thus an early American advocate of electoral reform declared, over a century ago (in language anticipating the most quoted passage of the *Reynolds v. Sims* opinion), "it is not land, nor owners of it, who form our constituencies, but the citizens generally." And the basic call of the English electoral-reform movement (echoed also in this country) was for "One Person, One Vote—One Vote, One Value." That, of course, was precisely the principle governing apportionments that the Supreme Court laid down in *Reynolds v. Sims*.

The most important thing about the *Baker v. Carr* and *Reynolds v. Sims* line of decisions to one interested in the Supreme Court is that, recent though those decisions may be, they are by now fully ingrained in our constitutional jurisprudence. And they have already begun to work a political readjustment, all but revolutionary in nature, which promises completely to alter the legislative power structure, so as to shift the legislative balance to the urban concentrations in which most Americans now live.

The provocative possibility in such an outcome is that it may lead to the revitalization of the legislative department itself, a revitalization that is so urgently needed if the representative democracy provided by the Framers is to survive. Not so long ago, during the Court-packing struggle of the mid-1930's, it was the Congress which preserved the Supreme Court as an effective judicial institution. Is it too fanciful to hope that, when all the ramifications of *Baker v. Carr* anid *Reynolds v. Sims* have been revealed, it will this time be the Court that has come to the rescue of the legislative department and furnished the catalyst for sorely needed legislative rejuvenation?

CHAPTER 11

Retrospect and Prospect

Strands and Pattern. The life of an institution such as the highest Court, like a piece of tapestry, is made up of many strands which, interwoven, make a pattern; to separate a single one and look at it alone not only destroys the whole but gives the strand itself a false value. All too many studies of the Supreme Court tend to overlook the institutional nature of that governmental organ. Small wonder, then, that the public has no clear picture of the working of our unique high judicial organ and of its proper place in a representative democracy. (*See Reading No. 20.*)

The Supreme Court is the only continuing governmental institution in our constitutional structure; individual justices may come and go, but their arrivals and departures scarcely affect the unbroken functioning of the Court as a judicial organ. Neophytes on the high bench—even the strongest of them—are immediately aware of the overpowering institutional traditions of the tribunal to which they have been elevated. Such awareness continues through the justices' professional life and, more than is generally realized, molds into the Court's pattern all but the most eccentric of its members. It has been said of Justice Brandeis that he had an almost mystic reverence for the Court, whose tradition seemed to him not only to consecrate its own members, but to impress its sacred mission upon all who shared in any measure in its work. Few members of the high tribunal may be capable of penetrating into its *mystique* with the perception of a Brandeis; still, all of them become, to greater or lesser extents, strongly imbued with its institutional traditions.

This view of the Court has been presented with the assumption that the pattern of the tapestry is more important than the single strands. Similarly, the Supreme Court as an institution is more significant than the individual justices who make up its membership. It is upon the Court as an institution that this history has primarily concentrated.

To be sure, to treat the high Court as an institutional entity may seem outdated in an age when even the law has succumbed to our society's preoccupation with the behavioristic sciences. Judges are only men, we are told—which is, of course, an indisputable observation. All the same, it hardly follows from this that it is only studies of the psychological makeups of the individual men who compose the Supreme Court that are now worthwhile. The state of a man's mind is as much a fact as the state of his digestion, according to the famous statement of a nineteenth century English judge. Now, however, we are told that the two are intimately related and that the state of a judge's mind can hardly be known without some knowledge of the state of his stomach. To advocates of this sort of gastrological jurisprudence, all attempts to describe the Court as an institutional entity are fundamentally naive.

No one not blind to the facts of legal life can deny that the Supreme Court in recent years has often presented a far from edifying spectacle of internal atomization. But even this has not prevented that tribunal from functioning as an institutional entity. The Supreme Court has been splintered before; still, the Court's work as a governmental organ has had to go on. It is a mistake to assume that, because the individual members of the tribunal are sharply divided, the Court has ceased to function as an institution. On the contrary, even amid a plethora of such cases, the institutional pattern continues to be woven. The present Court, like its predecessors, has been engaged in drawing the boundary at which conflicting interests are balanced; while it may still not be possible to determine such boundary by a general formula, points in the line have been fixed by decisions that this or that concrete case falls on the nearer or farther side. (*See Reading No. 21.*)

Retrospect. A survey of Supreme Court history is bound to reemphasize the crucial role which that tribunal has played in the development of the nation. More than that, it confirms the fact that the Court has, in the main, functioned as an institution that has served the needs of the American people. Writing over a century and a quarter ago, Justice Story declared that the universal sense of America had decided that there could be no Constitution without the Supreme Court. It is the Court which has, throughout our history, furnished an impartial tribunal to decide in the peaceful form of judicial proceedings controversies which, in other systems, are too frequently determined by the arbitrament of force. As Justice Jackson once put it, "Struggles over power that in Europe call out regiments of troops, in America call out regiments of lawyers."

It is true that there is always the danger in "government by lawsuit" of a judicial lag—of a gap between the changing needs of the times and the doctrines followed by the justices. Such a lag is, at times, inherent in a judicial tribunal which, because of the background and age of its members, may find it difficult to be a really contemporary institution. The Court in this sense may be the curb of a preceding generation upon the present one and may find it difficult to meet changing external conditions by fundamental modifications in its case law. The basic conservatism of a Court may prevent the necessary accommodation before it is too late. Mr. Dooley notwithstanding, the Supreme Court does not immediately follow the election returns.

Yet though there have been outstanding examples of judicial lag in our history (notably in the early New Deal period), it is erroneous to assume, as all too many writers have done, that the Court has been an institution that has frustrated effective government. On the contrary, if our survey of the Court's development has shown anything, it is how the main thrust of such development has met the felt needs of each period in the nation's history. While there have been aberrations, by and large the Court has remained true to Marshall's polestar—that we must never forget that "it is a *constitution* we are expounding," a living instrument that must be construed to meet the practical necessities of contemporary government.

At the outset, the primary needs of establishing national power on a firm basis and vindicating property rights against excesses of state power were met in the now-classic decisions of the Marshall Court. By Taney's day the needs of the society had changed. If the Taney Court was to translate the doctrines of Jacksonian democracy, and particularly its emphasis upon community rights, into constitutional law, that was true because such doctrines were deemed necessary to the proper development of the polity. In addition, they furthered the growth of corporate enterprise and prevented its restriction by the deadening hand of established monopoly. If in the latter part of the nineteenth century the Court was to elevate the rights of property to the plane of constitutional immunity, its due process decisions were the necessary legal accompaniment of the industrial conquest of a continent. The excesses of laissez-faire stimulated industrialism should not lead us to overlook the vital part it played in American development. Nor should it be forgotten that the Supreme Court decisions exalting property rights were a necessary accompaniment of the post-Civil War economic expansion.

In our own day the picture has become completely altered. We have come to recognize that property rights must be restricted to an extent never before permitted in our law. At the same time we have come to see that, unless the rights of the person are correlatively expanded, the individual will virtually be shorne of constitutional protection—hence in its recent jurisprudence the shift in Supreme Court emphasis to the protection of personal rights. The Court, like the rest of us, is disturbed by the growth of governmental authority and is seeking to preserve a sphere for individuality even in a society in which the individual stands dwarfed, if not overwhelmed, in the face of the power concentrations that confront him in the contemporary community.

Prospect. Not so long ago observers of the Supreme Court expected the 1937 "constitutional revolution" to signal a permanent decline in the Court's position. The basically subdued role played by it in the later New Deal period, during World War II, and in the early postwar years led many to expect the Supreme Court to wither away, much as the state was supposed to do in Marxist theory. Yet if one thing is clear it is that both the Soviet State and our high tribunal have anything but withered away in recent years. The Supreme Court has been as much in the headlines and the center of controversy during the past decade as it has ever been, and while this may hardly be a true criterion of its effectiveness, it surely shows the continued significance of the Court in the constitutional scheme of things.

What is true is that the work of the high Court today is different than it was in earlier periods. As seen in Chapter 10, the emphasis in the Court has shifted from the safeguarding of property rights to the protection of personal rights. Today, indeed, personal rights and liberties have become the very focus of the justices' contemporary constitutional concern. With the rights of property constitutionally curtailed, the Court has had to give compensatory scope to the rights of the person if the ultimate social interest—that in the individual life—was not to be lost sight of.

The need to broaden rather than curtail the Court's protection of personal rights has received added emphasis from the growth and misuse of governmental power in the twentieth century world. Those systems we disparagingly describe as totalitarian have shown us dramatically what it means for the individual to live in a society in which Leviathan has become a reality. As Justice Frankfurter has said, "The experience through which the world has passed in our own day has made vivid the realization that the Framers of our Constitution were not inexperienced doctrinaires." The "Blessings of Liberty," which the Framers took such pains to safeguard, have been placed in even sharper relief in a world which has so clearly seen the consequences of their extreme denial.

When the Constitution and the Bill of Rights were written, government was only an arbiter, allowing the individual to go unrestrained except when extreme limits of conduct were reached. In the century and a half that followed, there was a gradual shift from that system to one in which government had a positive duty to promote the welfare of the community, even at the cost of individual property rights. The transition was, as we saw, for a while impeded by the Supreme Court's construction of the due-process clause. Such narrow construction was, however, to give way in the face of changing conceptions of the proper governmental role. Under the jurisprudence of the present-day Court, governmental power may be exerted to further all the different social interests embraced in the ever-expanding notion of the public welfare. From a constitutional, as from a political, point of view, the Welfare State has been acknowledged as an established fact.

But the problem has ceased to be that of the exertion of governmental authority over property rights to further the public welfare. In the words of Justice Douglas, "the welfare state is a side issue. The central problem of the age is the scientific revolution and all the wonders and the damage it brings." The scientific revolution has created new concentrations of power, particularly in government, which utterly dwarf the individual and threaten, as never before, the very individuality which differentiates him from his fellows. "Where in this tightly knit regime," asks Douglas, "is man to find liberty?"

In its recent decisions protecting personal rights and liberties, the Supreme Court has responded to the felt necessities of the mid-twentieth century. And such response has enabled the Court to fashion for itself a constitutional role adapted to today's needs. Such role will continue to be vital in an age when the individual is in danger of being overwhelmed by concentrations of power.

Caveat. One cognizant of the values involved in the Bill of Rights cannot help but feel sympathetic toward the protective zeal recently shown by the Supreme Court. It is not, all the same, mere caviling to point out that judicial predisposition toward the libertarian result may be a two-edged sword. Properly employed, it can restore the essential balance between liberty and authority. Carried to its extreme, however, judicial libertarianism can lead the Court to assume undue authority over the other branches. This could make for a renaissance of the high tribunal as supreme censor of legislative and executive action—a role the Court has renounced ever since the "switch in time that saved nine" that effectively put an end to the Court-packing plan of the 1930's.

What was it that the Supreme Court had done in the years before 1937 to which much of the country objected so strongly? It was the erection by the justices of their personal predilections into constitutional dogmas which could not be touched by the legislature. It is true that the old Court's action in that respect was almost entirely limited to the economic field; yet that was so because it was in that field that legislative action was upsetting the justices' preconceptions.

Today none of the justices has difficulty in accepting governmental regulation that would have seemed all but revolutionary to the Court majority before 1937. In the economic area, then, deference to the other branches accords with the personal convictions of the present Court. The same is not true in the area of personal rights. Here, legislative restrictions run counter to the libertarian predispositions of most of the justices. But are these justices necessarily more justified in writing their private predilections into the Constitution than were their pre-1937 predecessors?

Consistency in a Court committed to the overriding values of democracy is not only consistency in seeking the libertarian result in all cases. Even restrictions on individual freedoms must be upheld when they are required for the preservation of other, more vital interests of society. If there is a danger in the recent tendency of the Warren Court, it is that the justices may overlook this and permit their personal libertarian convictions to override even necessary restrictions on individual rights.

It should not be forgotten that, no matter how we may gloss over it, judicial review is basically an undemocratic institution. Through the exercise of its review power the Supreme Court may enable the will even of the great majority of the people to be frustrated. That this is no mere theoretical possibility is shown by what actually happened in the pre-1937 period. The high bench then consistently set at naught policies of which most of the country approved, and it did so by resort to constitutional theories that we now see had clearly become outmoded. The Court is essentially a check of the past upon the present. But it is the present that represents the will of the people and it is that will that must ultimately be given effect in a democracy. If the democratic bases of our system are to be respected, the review power of the one nondemocratic organ in our government should be exercised with self-restraint.

It is paradoxical that it is those who profess to be the preachers of present-day liberalism who now assert the need for the Court to assume a more active responsibility in reviewing the constitutionality of legislative action. If there was one principle that nineteenth century liberals agreed upon, it was that of the primacy of legislative power. To them it was the elected representatives of the people, not an irresponsible judicial organ, who were endowed with primacy in the governmental structure. Yet whatever else we may think of the tenets of nineteenth century liberalism, is this not the proper distribution of governmental power in a representative democracy? Laws duly enacted by the people's representatives should not be aborted by judicial fiat unless the judges are presented with no other choice in the matter.

For the Court to assert again the degree of power it exercised prior to 1937 would be for it to deflect responsibility from those on whom in a democratic society it must ultimately rest—the people. As Chief Justice Marshall once said, "The people made the Constitution, and the people can unmake it. It is the creature of their will, and lives only by their will." It is the Supreme Court's ultimate responsibility to see that their will is faithfully executed in the determination of controversies.

Courts are not the only instruments of government that can be relied upon to preserve us against harm. If they were, they would be largely inadequate for the purpose. Civil liberties can at best draw only limited strength from judicial guarantees. Courts can hardly be expected by themselves to preserve us against our own excesses. It is no idle speculation to inquire which comes first, judicial enforcement of constitutional rights or a free and tolerant society. Must we, in Justice Jackson's question, first maintain a system of free government to assure a free and independent judiciary, or can we rely upon an aggressive, activist judiciary to guarantee free government? Americans not infrequently forget the answer to this question. Without a doubt, the Supreme Court is of basic importance, particularly in molding public opinion to accept fully the implications of the rule of law; the law enunciated by it may have a definite educative as well as a normative effect. But it is the attitude of the society and of its organized political forces, rather than of its purely legal machinery alone, that must remain the controlling force in the character of free institutions. (*See Reading No. 22.*)

Part II
READINGS

READING NO. 1

George Washington on Judicial Appointments, 1789*

The importance of Supreme Court appointments has been recognized from the founding of the Republic, as is shown by these letters of the first President. The first is the famous letter to the first Attorney General, Edmund Randolph; the others to the first Supreme Court appointees. Despite Washington's clear comprehension of the responsibility of making suitable appointments to the first Court, he found it most difficult to get men of stature to accept. The low prestige of the Court led a number of his first choices to prefer other positions.

New York, 27 September, 1789.

Dear Sir,

Impressed with a conviction, that the due administration of justice is the firmest pillar of good government, I have considered the first arrangement of the judicial department as essential to the happiness of our country, and to the stability of its political system. Hence the selection of the fittest characters to expound the laws, and dispense justice, has been an invariable object of my anxious concern.

I mean not to flatter when I say, that considerations like these have ruled in the nomination of the attorney-general of the United States, and that my private wishes would be highly gratified by your acceptance of the office. I regarded the office as requiring those talents to conduct its important duties, and that disposition to make sacrifices to the public good, which I believe you to possess and entertain. In both instances I doubt not the event will justify the conclusion. The appointment I hope will be accepted, and its functions, I am assured, will be well performed.

* *The Writings of George Washington,* Vol. 10 (Sparks ed., New York, 1847), pp. 34-6.

Notwithstanding the prevailing disposition to frugality, the salary of this office appears to have been fixed at what it is, from a belief that the station would confer preëminence on its possessor, and procure for him a decided preference of professional employment. As soon as the acts, which are necessary accompaniments of the appointment, can be got ready, you will receive official notice of the latter. This letter is only to be considered as an early communication of my sentiments on this occasion, and as a testimony of the sincere regard and esteem, with which I am, &c.

To the Associate Judges of the Supreme Court.

New York, 30 September, 1789.

Sir,

I experience peculiar pleasure in giving you notice of your appointment to the office of an associate judge in the Supreme Court of the United States.

Considering the judicial system as the chief pillar upon which our national government must rest, I have thought it my duty to nominate for the high offices in that department, such men as I conceived would give dignity and lustre to our national character; and I flatter myself that the love, which you bear to our country, and a desire to promote the general happiness, will lead you to a ready acceptance of the enclosed commission, which is accompanied with such laws as have passed relative to your office. I have the honor to be, with high consideration, &c.

To John Jay.

New York, 5 October, 1789

Sir,

It is with singular pleasure, that I address you as Chief Justice of the Supreme Court of the United States, for which office your commission is enclosed.

In nominating you for the important station, which you now fill, I not only acted in conformity to my best judgment, but I trust I did a grateful thing to the good citizens of these United States; and I have a full confidence, that the love which you bear to our country, and a desire to promote the general happiness, will not suffer you to hesitate a moment to bring into action the talents, knowledge, and integrity, which are so necessary to be exercised at the head of that department, which must be considered as the key-stone of our political fabric. I have the honor to be, with high consideration and sentiments of esteem, &c.

READING NO. 2

Minutes of the Supreme Court's First Sessions, 1790*

The official minutes of the Court's first sessions are of more than antiquarian interest, for they strikingly demonstrate the lack of business in the first Court. Curiously, the very first line in the minutes contains an error in the Court's title; the Court's clerk was from Massachusetts and (probably subconsciously) used the title of that state's highest court, Supreme Judicial Court.

At the Supreme Judicial Court of the United States, begun and held at New York (being the Seat of the National Government), on the first Monday of February, and on the first day of said month Anno Domini 1790.

Present

The Honble John Jay Esquire   Chief Justice

The Honble William Cushing, and James Wilson, Esqrs.
    Associate Justices.

This being the day assigned by Law, for commencing the first Sessions of the Supreme Court of the United States, and a sufficient Number of the Justices not being convened, the Court is adjourned, by the Justices now present, untill to Morrow, at one of the Clock in the afternoon.

* *The American Journal of Legal History,* Vol. 5 (Philadelphia, 1961), pp. 69-71.

THE SUPREME COURT'S FIRST SESSIONS

Tuesday, February 2nd 1790.

Present

The Honble John Jay Esq.   Chief Justice

The Honble William Cushing, James Wilson and John Blair, Esqs.
  Associate Justices

Proclamation is made and the Court is opened.

Letters patent to the Honble John Jay Esquire, bearing date the 26th day of September 1789, appointing him Chief Justice, of the Supreme Court of the United States, are openly read, and published in Court.

Letters patent to the Honble William Cushing, Esquire, bearing date the 27th day of September 1789 appointing him associate Justice of the Supreme Court of the United States are openly read and published in Court.

Letters patent to the Honble James Wilson, Esquire, bearing date the 29th day of September 1789 appointing him Associate Justice of the Supreme Court of the United States, are openly read and published in Court.

Letters patent to the Honble John Blair Esquire bearing date the 30th day of September 1789, appointing him Associate Justice of the Supreme Court of the United States, are openly read and published in Court.

Letters patent to Edmond Randolph of Virginia, Esqr., bearing date the 26th day of September 1789, appointing him Attorney General for the United States are open[ly] read and published in Court.

Ordered, that Richard Wenman, be, and he is appointed Cryer of this Court.

Adjourned untill to morrow at one of the Clock in the Afternoon.

Wednesday February 3rd 1790

Present

The Honble John Jay, Esquire   Chief Justice

The Honble William Cushing, James Wilson and John Blair, Esquires   Associate Justices

Proclamation is made and the Court is opened.

Ordered, that John Tucker Esq. of Boston be the Clerk of this Court. That he reside, and keep his Office at the Seat of the National Government, and that he do not practice either as an Attorney or a Counsellor in this Court while he shall continue to be Clerk of the same.

The said John Tucker in open Court, takes the Oath of Office by Law prescribed to be taken by the Clerk of the Court, and an Oath to Support the Constitution of the United States: and also gives Bond approved of by this Court, to the United States, for the faithful discharge of his Duty as Clerk aforesaid, as by Law required.

Ordered, that the Seal of this Court shall be the Arms of the United States, engraved on a circular piece of Steel of the Size of a Dollar, with these words in the Margin "The Seal of the Supreme Court of the United States." And that the Seals of the Circuit Courts shall be the Arms of the United States engraven on circular pieces of Silver of the Size of half a dollar, with these words in the Margin Viz. In the upper part "the Seal of the circuit Court, in the lower part the name of the District for which it is intended.

Ordered, that the Clerk of the Court cause the before mentioned Seals to be made accordingly; and when done that he convey those for the Circuit Court to the district Clerk respectivily.

Adjourned to Friday the fifth day of February 1790.

READING NO. 3

The Court on Advisory Opinions, July 20 and August 8, 1793*

In 1793 President Washington, through a letter sent to the justices by Secretary of State Jefferson, sought the advice of the Supreme Court on a series of troublesome "abstract questions" in the realm of international law "which have already occurred, or may soon occur." Chief Justice Jay and his associates first postponed their answer until the sitting of the Court and then, three weeks later, replied politely, but firmly, declining to give the requested answers—a refusal that has served as a precedent against the giving of advisory opinions by the high Court.

A.

Philadelphia, 20th July, 1793.

Sir:

We have taken into consideration the letter written to us, by your direction, on the 18th inst., by the Secretary of State. The question, "whether the public may, with propriety, be availed of the advice of the judges on the questions alluded to," appears to us to be of much difficulty as well as importance. As it affects the judicial department, we feel a reluctance to decide it without the advice and participation of our absent brethren.

The occasion which induced our being convened is doubtless urgent; of the degree of that urgency we cannot judge, and consequently cannot propose that the answer to this question be postponed until the sitting of the Supreme Court. We are not only disposed, but desirous, to promote the welfare of our country in every way that may consist with our official duties. We are pleased, sir, with every opportunity of manifesting our respect for you, and are solicitous to do whatever may be in our power

---

* *The Correspondence and Public Papers of John Jay*, Vol. 3 (Johnston ed., New York, 1891), pp. 487-9.

to render your administration as easy and agreeable to yourself as it is to our country. If circumstances should forbid further delay, we will immediately resume the consideration of the question, and decide it.

We have the honour to be, with perfect respect, your most obedient and most humble servants.

B.

Philadelphia, 8th August, 1793.

Sir:

We have considered the previous question stated in a letter written by your direction to us by the Secretary of State on the 18th of last month, [regarding] the lines of separation drawn by the Constitution between the three departments of the government. These being in certain respects checks upon each other, and our being judges of a court in the last resort, are considerations which afford strong arguments against the propriety of our extra-judicially deciding the questions alluded to, especially as the power given by the Constitution to the President, of calling on the heads of departments for opinions, seems to have been *purposely* as well as expressly united to the *executive* departments.

We exceedingly regret every event that may cause embarrassment to your administration, but we derive consolation from the reflection that your judgment will discern what is right, and that your usual prudence, decision, and firmness will surmount every obstacle to the preservation of the rights, peace, and dignity of the United States.

We have the honour to be, with perfect respect, sir, your most obedient and most humble servants.

READING NO. 4

John Marshall's Autobiographical Letter, 1827*

This recently discovered sketch of Marshall's early life, the most complete to come from his pen, was written to Justice Joseph Story when the great Chief Justice was seventy-two years old. It contains a rare personal account of Marshall the man that is absent from accounts of his career, notably in Beveridge's classic biography. The meagerness of Marshall's pre-Supreme Court training makes us wonder, all the more, at his masterful opinions which provided a doctrinal base for the new nation.

My Dear Sir:

The events of my life are too unimportant, and have too little interest for any person not of my immediate family, to render them worth communicating or preserving. I felt therefore some difficulty in commencing their detail, since the mere act of detailing, exhibits the appearance of attaching consequence to them;—a difficulty which was not overcome till the receipt of your favour of the 14th inst. If I conquer it now, it is because the request is made by a partial and highly valued friend.

I was born on the 24th of Septr. 1755 in the county of Fauquier at that time one of the frontier counties of Virginia. My father possessed scarcely any fortune, and had received a very limited education;—but was a man to whom nature had been bountiful, and who had assiduously improved her gifts. He superintended my education, and gave me an early taste for history and for poetry. At the age of twelve I had transcribed Pope's essay on man, with some of his moral essays.

There being at that time no grammar school in the part of the country in which my Father resided I was sent, at fourteen, about one hundred miles from home, to be placed under the

* *An Autobiographical Sketch by John Marshall* (Adams ed., Ann Arbor, 1937), pp. 3-5, 6-7, 12, 20, 25-26, 29-32.

tuition of Mr. Campbell a clergyman of great respectability. I remained with him one year, after which I was brought home and placed under the care of a Scotch gentleman who was just introduced into the parish as Pastor, and who resided in my Fathers family. He remained in the family one year, at the expiration of which time I had commenced reading Horace and Livy. I continued my studies with no other aid than my Dictionary. My Father superintended the English part of my education, and to his care I am indebted for anything valuable which I may have acquired in my youth. He was my only intelligent companion; and was both a watchfull parent and an affectionate instructive friend. The young men within my reach were entirely uncultivated; and the time I passed with them was devoted to hardy athletic exercises.

About the time I entered my eighteenth year, the controversy between Great Britain and her colonies had assumed so serious an aspect as almost to monopolize the attention of the old and the young. I engaged in it with all the zeal and enthusiasm which belonged to my age; and devoted more time to learning the first rudiments of military exercise in an Independent company of the gentlemen of the county, to training a militia company in the neighbourhood, and to the political essays of the day, than to the classics or to Blackstone.

In the summer of 1775 I was appointed a first lieutenant in a company of minute men designed for actual service. . . .

As that part of the Virginia line which had not marched to Charleston was dissolving by the expiration of the terms for which the men had enlisted, the officers were directed to return home in the winter of 1779-80, in order to take charge of such men as the legislature should raise for them. I availed myself of this inactive interval for attending a course of law lectures given by Mr. Wythe, and of lectures of Natural philosophy given by Mr. Madison then President of William and Mary College. The vacation commenced in july when I left the university, and obtained a license to practice law. In October I returned to the army, and continued in service until the termination of Arnolds invasion after which, in February 1781, before the invasion of Phillips, there being a redundancy of officers, I resigned my commission. I had formed a strong attachment to the young lady whom I afterwards married; and as we had more officers than soldiers, thought I might without violating the duty I owed my country, pay some attention to my future prospects in life.

It was my design to go immediately to the bar; but the invasion of Virginia soon took place, and the courts were closed till the capitulation of Lord Cornwallis. After that event the courts were opened and I commenced practice. . . .

Colonel Griffin named me to General Washington as the attorney for the district, an office which I had wished, but I declined accepting it because at that time the circuit courts of the United States were held at two distinct places far apart, and distant from the seat of government where the superior courts of the state sat. Consequently I could not attend them regularly without some detriment to my state practice. Before this inconvenience was removed the office was conferred on another gentleman. . . .

It was about or perhaps a little after this time that I was invited by General Washington to take the office of Attorney General of the United States. I was too deeply engaged in the practice in Virginia to accept this office, though I should certainly have preferred it to any other. . . .

I returned to Richmond with a full determination to devote myself entirely to my professional duties, and was not a little delighted to find that my prospects at the bar had sustained no material injury from my absence. My friends welcomed my return with the most flattering reception, and pressed me to become a candidate for Congress. My refusal was peremptory, and I did not believe it possible that my determination could be shaken. I was however mistaken.

General Washington gave a pressing invitation to his nephew, the present Judge, & myself, to pass a few days at Mount Vernon. He urged us both very earnestly to come into Congress & Mr. Washington assented to his wishes. I resisted, on the ground of my situation, & the necessity of attending to my pecuniary affairs. I can never forget the manner in which he treated this objection.

He said there were crises in national affairs which made it the duty of a citizen to forego his private for the public interest. We were then in one of them. He detailed his opinions freely on the nature of our controversy with France and expressed his conviction that the best interests of our country depended on the character of the ensuing Congress. He concluded a very earnest conversation, one of the most interesting I was ever engaged in, by asking my attention to his situation. He had retired from the Executive department with the firmest determination never again to appear in a public capacity. He had communicated this determination to the public, and his motives for adhering to it were too strong not to be well understood. Yet I saw him pledged to appear once more at the head of the American army. What must be his convictions of duty imposed by the present state of American affairs?

I yielded to his representations & became a candidate. I soon afterwards received a letter from the Secretary of state offering me the seat on the bench of the supreme court which had become vacant by the death of Judge Iredell; but my preference for the bar still continued & I declined it. . . .

On the resignation of Chief Justice Ellsworth I recommended Judge Patteson [*sic*] as his successor. The President objected to him, and assigned as his ground of objection that the feelings of Judge Cushing would be wounded by passing him and selecting a junior member of the bench. I never heard him assign any other objection to Judge Patteson, though it was afterwards suspected by many that he was believed to be connected with the party which opposed the second attempt at negotiation with France. The President himself mentioned Mr. Jay, and he was nominated to the senate. When I waited on the President with Mr. Jays letter declining the appointment he said thoughtfully "Who shall I nominate now"? I replied that I could not tell, as I supposed that his objection to Judge Patteson remained. He said in a decided tone "I shall not nominate him." After a moments hesitation he said "I believe I must nominate you". I had never before heard myself named for the office and had not even thought of it. I was pleased as well as surprized, and bowed in silence. Next day I was nominated, and, although the nomination was suspended by the friends of Judge Patteson, it was I believe when taken up unanimously approved. I was unfeignedly gratified at the appointment, and have had much reason to be so. I soon received a very friendly letter from Judge Patteson congratulating me on the occasion and expressing [his] hopes that I might long retain the office. I felt truely grateful for the real cordiality towards me which uniformly marked his conduct.

I have my dear Sir been much more minute and tedious in detail than the occasion required, but you will know how to prune, condense, exclude, and vary. I give you the materials of which you will make some thing or nothing as you please— taking this only with you, that you will be sure to gratify me by pursuing precisely the tract you had marked out for yourself, & admitting nothing which may overload the narrative according to the original plan. Do not insert any thing from the suspicion that I may look for it because I have introduced it into my narrative.

It would seem as if new and perplexing questions on jurisdiction will never be exhausted. That which you mention is one of the strongest possible illustrations, so far as respects the original act, of the necessity in some instances of controuling the letter by the plain spirit of the law. It is impossible that a suit brought by the U.S. can be within the intention of the exception. There is however great difficulty in taking the case out of the letter. The argument you state is very strong and I am much inclined to yield to it. As no private citizen can sue in a district court on a promissory note I am much inclined to restrain the exception to those district courts which have circuit court jurisdiction. But the difficulty is I think removed by the act of the 3d of March 1815 and by the decision of the last term. I speak of that decision however from memory as I have not yet received 12th Wheaton.

Farewell—with the highest respect & esteem

I am yours
J Marshall

READING NO. 5

Marbury v. Madison, 1803*

This, the most famous case decided by the Marshall Court, established the Supreme Court's authority to review the constitutionality of statutes. As such, it is rightly considered the cornerstone of the American constitutional system. The opinion shows Marshall at his magisterial best, with the developing momentum of his argument marching with measured cadence to its inevitable logical conclusion. It was of such a masterful performance that one of Marshall's opponents despairingly commented, "All wrong, all wrong, but no man in the United States can tell why or wherein."

On the 24th February, the following opinion of the court was delivered by the Chief Justice: . . .

In the order in which the court has viewed this subject, the following questions have been considered and decided: 1st. Has the applicant a right to the commission he demands? 2d. If he has a right, and that right has been violated, do the laws of his country afford him a remedy? 3d. If they do afford him a remedy, is it a *mandamus* issuing from this court? . . .

It is, then, the opinion of the Court: 1st. That by signing the commission of Mr. Marbury, the President of the United States appointed him a justice of peace for the county of Washington, in the district of Columbia; and that the seal of the United States, affixed thereto by the secretary of state, is conclusive testimony of the verity of the signature, and of the completion of the appointment; and that the appointment conferred on him a legal right to the office for the space of five years. 2d. That, having this legal title to the office, he has a consequent right to the commission; a refusal to deliver which is a plain violation of that right, for which the laws of his country afford him a remedy.

* 1 Cranch 137, 152-80 (U.S. 1803).

3. It remains to be inquired whether he is entitled to the remedy for which he applies? . . .

This, then, is a plain case for a *mandamus*, either to deliver the commission, or a copy of it from the record; and it only remains to be inquired, whether it can issue from this court?

The act to establish the judicial courts of the United States authorizes the supreme court, "to issue writs of *mandamus*, in cases warranted by the principles and usages of law, to any courts appointed or persons holding office, under the authority of the United States." The secretary of state, being a person holding an office under the authority of the United States, is precisely within the letter of this description; and if this court is not authorized to issue a writ of *mandamus* to such an officer, it must be because the law is unconstitutional, and therefore, absolutely incapable of conferring the authority, and assigning the duties which its words purport to confer and assign. . . .

The question, whether an act, repugnant to the constitution, can become the law of the land, is a question deeply interesting to the United States; but, happily, not of an intricacy proportioned to its interest. It seems only necessary to recognize certain principles, supposed to have been long and well established, to decide it. That the people have an original right to establish, for their future government, such principles as, in their opinion, shall most conduce to their own happiness, is the basis on which the whole American fabric has been erected. The exercise of this original right is a very great exertion; nor can it, nor ought it, to be frequently repeated. The principles, therefore, so established, are deemed fundamental: and as the authority from which they proceed is supreme, and can seldom act, they are designed to be permanent.

This original and supreme will organizes the government, and assigns to different departments their respective powers. It may either stop here, or establish certain limits not to be transcended by those departments. The government of the United States is of the latter description. The powers of the legislature are defined and limited; and that those limits may not be mistaken or forgotten, the constitution is written. To what purpose are powers limited, and to what purpose is that limitation committed to writing, if these limits may, at any time, be passed by those intended to be restrained? The distinction between a government with limited and unlimited powers is abolished, if those limits do not confine the persons on whom they are imposed, and if acts prohibited and acts allowed, are of equal obligation. It is a proposition too plain to be contested, that the constitution controls any legislative act repugnant to it; or that the legislature may alter the constitution by an ordinary act.

Between these alternatives, there is no middle ground. The constitution is either a superior paramount law, unchangeable by ordinary means, or it is on a level with ordinary legislative acts, and, like other acts, is alterable when the legislature shall please to alter it. If the former part of the alternative be true, then a legislative act, contrary to the constitution, is not law: if the latter part be true, then written constitutions are absurd attempts, on the part of the people, to limit a power, in its own nature, illimitable.

Certainly, all those who have framed written constitutions contemplate them as forming the fundamental and paramount law of the nation, and consequently, the theory of every such government must be, that an act of the legislature, repugnant to the constitution, is void. This theory is essentially attached to a written constitution, and is, consequently, to be considered, by this court, as one of the fundamental principles of our society. It is not, therefore, to be lost sight of, in the further consideration of this subject.

If an act of the legislature, repugnant to the constitution, is void, does it, notwithstanding its invalidity, bind the courts, and oblige them to give it effect? Or, in other words, though it be not law, does it constitute a rule as operative as if it was a law? This would be to overthrow, in fact, what was established in theory; and would seem, at first view, an absurdity too gross to be insisted on. It shall, however, receive a more attentive consideration.

It is, emphatically, the province and duty of the judicial department, to say what the law is. Those who apply the rule to particular cases, must of necessity expound and interpret that rule. If two laws conflict with each other, the courts must decide on the operation of each. So, if a law be in opposition to the constitution; if both the law and the constitution apply to a particular case, so that the court must either decide that case, conformable to the law, disregarding the constitution; or conformable to the constitution, disregarding the law; the court must determine which of these conflicting rules governs the case: this is of the very essence of judicial duty. If then, the courts are to regard the constitution, and the constitution is superior to any ordinary act of the legislature, the constitution, and not such ordinary act, must govern the case to which they both apply.

Those, then, who controvert the principle, that the constitution is to be considered, in court, as a paramount law, are reduced to the necessity of maintaining that courts must close their eyes on the constitution, and see only the law. This doctrine would subvert the very foundation of all written constitutions. It would declare that an act which, according to the principles and theory of our government, is entirely void, is yet, in practice, completely obligatory. It would declare, that if the legislature shall do what is expressly forbidden, such act, notwithstanding the express prohibition, is in reality effectual. It would be giving to the legislature a practical and real omnipotence with the same breath which professes to restrict their powers within narrow limits. It is prescribing limits, and declaring that those limits may be passed at pleasure. That it thus reduces to nothing, what we have deemed the greatest improvement on political institutions, a written constitution, would, of itself, be sufficient, in America, where written constitutions have been viewed with so much reverence, for rejecting the construction. But the peculiar expressions of the constitution of the United States furnish additional arguments in favor of its rejection. The judicial power of the United States is extended to all cases arising under the constitution. Could it be the intention of those who gave this power, to say, that in using it, the constitution should not be looked into? That a case arising under the constitution should be decided, without examining the instrument under which it arises? This is too extravagant to be maintained. In some cases, then, the constitution must be looked into by the judges. And if they can open it at all, what part of it are they forbidden to read or to obey?

There are many other parts of the constitution which serve to illustrate this subject. It is declared, that "no tax or duty shall be laid on articles exported from any state." Suppose, a duty on the export of cotton, of tobacco or of flour; and a suit instituted to recover it. Ought judgment to be rendered in such a case? ought the judges to close their eyes on the constitution, and only see the law?

The constitution declares "that no bill of attainder or *ex post facto* law shall be passed." If, however, such a bill should be passed, and a person should be prosecuted under it; must the court condemn to death those victims whom the constitution endeavors to preserve?

"No person," says the constitution, "shall be convicted of treason, unless on the testimony of two witnesses to the same *overt* act, or on confession in open court." Here, the language of the constitution is addressed especially to the courts. It prescribes, directly for them, a rule of evidence not to be departed from. If the legislature should change that rule, and declare one witness, or a confession out of court, sufficient for conviction, must the constitutional principle yield to the legislative act?

From these, and many other selections which might be made, it is apparent, that the framers of the constitution contemplated that instrument as a rule for the government of courts, as well as of the legislature. Why otherwise does it direct the judges to take an oath to support it? This oath certainly applies in an especial manner, to their conduct in their official character. How immoral to impose it on them, if they were to be used as the instruments, and the knowing instruments, for violating what they swear to support!

The oath of office, too, imposed by the legislature, is completely demonstrative of the legislative opinion on this subject. It is in these words: "I do solemnly swear, that I will administer justice, without respect to persons, and do equal right to the poor and to the rich; and that I will faithfully and impartially discharge all the duties incumbent on me as————, according to the best of my abilities and understanding, agreeably to the constitution and laws of the United States." Why does a judge swear to discharge his duties agreeably to the constitution of the United States, if that constitution forms no rule for his government? if it is closed upon him, and cannot be inspected by him? If such be the real state of things, this is worse than solemn mockery. To prescribe, or to take this oath, becomes equally a crime.

It is also not entirely unworthy of the observation, that in declaring what shall be the supreme law of the land, the constitution itself is first mentioned; and not the laws of the United States, generally, but those only which shall be made in pursuance of the constitution, have that rank.

Thus, the particular phraseology of the constitution of the United States confirms and strengthens the principle, supposed to be essential to all written constitutions, that a law repugnant to the constitution is void; and that courts, as well as other departments, are bound by that instrument.

The rule must be discharged.

READING NO. 6

Thomas Jefferson on Judicial Review, September 6, 1819*

According to Charles Warren, "To the public of 1803, [Marbury v. Madison] represented the determination of Marshall and his Associates to interfere with the authority of the Executive." Marshall's assertion of review power in the Court was bitterly opposed by Jefferson, who was actually the chief target of the strictures in Marshall's opinion. This letter, written a decade and a half after Marbury v. Madison, *shows Jefferson's continued feelings in the matter. It is of particular interest because it was written to Judge Spencer Roane of Virginia, who would have been Jefferson's own choice to head the Supreme Court, had the vacancy which Marshall filled occurred only two months later.*

. . . I subscribe to every tittle of them. They contain the true principles of the revolution of 1800, for that was as real a revolution in the principles of our government as that of 76 was in its form; not effected indeed by the sword . . . the nation declared it's will by dismissing functionaries of one principle, and electing those of another, in the two branches, executive and legislative, submitted to their election. Over the judiciary department, the constitution had deprived them of their control. That therefore has continued the reprobated system. . . . [The Constitution provides a group of departments] coordinate and independent, that they might check and balance one another. It has given, according to this opinion, to one of them alone the right to prescribe rules for the government of the others; and to that one too which is unelected by, and, independent of, the nation, for experience has already shewn that the impeachment it has provided is not even a scare crow. . . . The constitution, on this

* *The Writings of Thomas Jefferson,* Vol. 10 (Ford ed., New York, 1899), pp. 140-43 hypothesis is a mere thing of wax in the hands of the judiciary, which they may twist and shape into any form they please. It should be remembered as an axiom of eternal truth in politics that whatever power in any government is independent, is absolute also. . . . My construction of the constitution is very different from that you quote. It is that each department is truly independent of the others and has an equal right to decide for itself what is the meaning of the constitution in the cases submitted to it's action. . . . I will explain myself by examples which, having occurred while I was in office, are better known to me. . . .

A legislature had past the Sedition law, the federal courts had subjected certain individuals to it's penalties, of fine and imprisonment. On coming into office I released these individuals by the power of pardon committed to Executive direction, which could never be more properly exercised than where citizens were suffering without the authority of law, or, which was equivalent, under a law unauthorized by the constitution, & therefore null. In the case of Marbury and Madison, the federal judges declared that commissions, signed and sealed by the President, were valid, altho' not delivered. I deemed delivery essential to compleat a deed, which, as long as it remains in the hands of the party, is as yet no deed, it is in posse only, but not in esse, and I withheld delivery of the Commissions. They cannot issue a Mandamus to the President or legislature, or to any of their officers. When the British treaty of 180- arrived, without any provision against the impressment of our seamen, I determined not to ratify it. The Senate thought I should ask their advice. I thought that would be a mockery of them when I was predetermined against following it should they advise it's ratification. The constitution had made their advice necessary to confirm a treaty, but not to reject it. This has been blamed by some, but I never doubted it's soundness. . . .

These are examples of my position that each of the three departments has equally the right to decide for itself what is it's duty, under the constitution, without any regard to what the others may have decided for themselves under a similar question. But you intimate a wish that my opinion should be known on this subject. No, dear Sir, I withdrew from all contests of opinion, and resign everything chearfully to the generation now in place. They are wiser than we were, and their successors will be wiser than them from the progressive advance of science. Tranquility is the summum bonum of age. I wish therefore to offend no man's opinions nor to draw disquieting animadversions on my own. While duty required it I met opposition with a firm and fearless step, but loving mankind in my individual relations with them I pray to be permitted to depart in their peace; and like the superannuated soldier . . . to hang my arms on the post. . . .

READING NO. 7

Andrew Jackson's Veto Message, 1832*

In 1832 Congress passed a bill to renew the charter of the Bank of the United States. President Jackson met the bill with a categorical veto. The political and economic issues involved in the Bank controversy, crucial though they were at the time, are now of interest primarily to Jacksonian specialists. But the veto message, drafted in large part by soon-to-be Chief Justice Taney, deserves rereading. The core of the message was, of course, Jackson's hostility to the Bank and his ringing statement of the rights of the common man. To us, however, the veto is noteworthy for its assertion (written by the man who was to be Marshall's successor) of power in the President to review a constitutional question already decided by the Supreme Court.

Washington, *July 10, 1832.*

To the Senate:

The bill "to modify and continue" the act entitled "An act to incorporate the subscribers to the Bank of the United States" was presented to me on the 4th July instant. Having considered it with that solemn regard to the principles of the Constitution which the day was calculated to inspire, and come to the conclusion that it ought not to become a law, I herewith return it to the Senate in which it originated, with my objections. . . .

It is maintained by the advocates of the bank that its constitutionality in all its features ought to be considered as settled by precedent and by the decision of the Supreme Court. To this conclusion I can not assent. Mere precedent is a dangerous source of authority, and should not be regarded as deciding questions of constitutional power except where the acquiescence of the people and the States can be considered as well settled. So far from this being the case on this subject, an argument against the

* J. D. Richardson, *A Compilation of the Messages and Papers of the Presidents,* Vol. 2 (Washington, 1897), pp. 576-91.

113

bank might be based on precedent. One Congress, in 1791, decided in favor of a bank; another, in 1811, decided against it. One Congress, in 1815, decided against a bank; another, in 1816, decided in its favor. Prior to the present Congress, therefore, the precedents drawn from that source were equal. If we resort to the States, the expressions of legislative, judicial, and executive opinions against the bank have been probably to those in its favor as 4 to 1. There is nothing in precedent, therefore, which, if its authority were admitted, ought to weigh in favor of the act before me.

If the opinion of the Supreme Court covered the whole ground of this act, it ought not to control the coordinate authorities of this Government. The Congress, the Executive, and the Court must each for itself be guided by its own opinion of the Constitution. Each public officer who takes an oath to support the Constitution swears that he will support it as he understands it, and not as it is understood by others. It is as much the duty of the House of Representatives, of the Senate, and of the President to decide upon the constitutionality of any bill or resolution which may be presented to them for passage or approval as it is of the supreme judges when it may be brought before them for judicial decision. The opinion of the judges has no more authority over Congress than the opinion of Congress has over the judges, and on that point the President is independent of both. The authority of the Supreme Court must not, therefore, be permitted to control the Congress or the Executive when acting in their legislative capacities, but to have only such influence as the force of their reasoning may deserve.

But in the case relied upon the Supreme Court have not decided that all the features of this corporation are compatible with the Constitution. It is true that the court have said that the law incorporating the bank is a constitutional exercise of power by Congress; but taking into view the whole opinion of the court and the reasoning by which they have come to that conclusion, I understand them to have decided that inasmuch as a bank is an appropriate means for carrying into effect the enumerated powers of the General Government, therefore the law incorporating it is in accordance with that provision of the Constitution which declares that Congress shall have power "to make all laws which shall be necessary and proper for carrying those powers into execution." Having satisfied themselves that the word *"necessary"* in the Constitution means *"needful," "requisite," "essential," "conducive to,"* and that "a bank" is a convenient, a useful, and essential instrument in the prosecution of the Government's "fiscal operations," they conclude that to "use one must be within the discretion of Congress" and that "the act to incorporate the Bank of the United States is a law made in pursuance of the Constitution;" "but," say they, *"where the law is not prohibited and is really calculated to effect any of the objects intrusted to the Government, to undertake here to inquire into the degree of its necessity would be to pass the line which circumscribes the judicial department and to tread on legislative ground."*

The principle here affirmed is that the "degree of its necessity," involving all the details of a banking institution, is a question exclusively for legislative consideration. A bank is constitutional, but it is the province of the Legislature to determine whether this or that particular power, privilege, or exemption is "necessary and proper" to enable the bank to discharge its duties to the Goverment, and from their decision there is no appeal to the courts of justice. Under the decision of the Supreme Court, therefore, it is the exclusive province of Congress and the President to decide whether the particular features of this act are *necessary* and *proper* in order to enable the bank to perform conveniently and efficiently the public duties assigned to it as a fiscal agent, and therefore constitutional, or *unnecessary* and *improper*, and therefore unconstitutional. . . .

The bank is professedly established as an agent of the executive branch of the Government, and its constitutionality is maintained on that ground. Neither upon the propriety of present action nor upon the provisions of this act was the Executive consulted. It has had no opportunity to say that it neither needs nor wants an agent clothed with such powers and favored by such exemptions. There is nothing in its legitimate functions which makes it necessary or proper. Whatever interest or influence, whether public or private, has given birth to this act, it can not be found either in the wishes or necessities of the executive department, by which present action is deemed premature, and the powers conferred upon its agent not only unnecessary, but dangerous to the Government and country.

It is to be regretted that the rich and powerful too often bend the acts of government to their selfish purposes. Distinctions in society will always exist under every just government. Equality of talents, of education, or of wealth can not be produced by human institutions. In the full enjoyment of the gifts of Heaven and the fruits of superior industry, economy, and virtue, every man is equally entitled to protection by law; but when the laws undertake to add to these natural and just advantages artificial distinctions, to grant titles, gratuities, and exclusive privileges, to make the rich richer and the potent more powerful, the humble members of society—the farmers, mechanics, and laborers—who have neither the time nor the means of securing like favors to themselves, have a right to complain of the injustice of their Government. There are no necessary evils in government. Its evils exist only in its abuses. If it would confine itself to equal protection, and, as Heaven does its rains, shower its favors alike on the high and the low, the rich and the poor, it would be an unqualified blessing. In the act before me there seems to be a wide and unnecessary departure from these just principles. . . .

I have now done my duty to my country. If sustained by my fellow-citizens, I shall be grateful and happy; if not, I shall find in the motives which impel me ample grounds for contentment and peace. In the difficulties which surround us and the dangers which threaten our institutions there is cause for neither dismay nor alarm. For relief and deliverance let us firmly rely on that kind Providence which I am sure watches with peculiar care over the destinies of our Republic, and on the intelligence and wisdom of our countrymen. Through *His* abundant goodness and *their* patriotic devotion our liberty and Union will be preserved.

ANDREW JACKSON.

READING NO. 8

Charles River Bridge v. Warren Bridge, 1837*

The accession of Chief Justice Taney and other Jackson appointees resulted in a change in emphasis on the constitutional protection given to property rights. Such change was first articulated in Taney's opinion in this case—the first important case decided after Marshall's death. It should be noted, however, that the Taney decision actually helped economic development, for, while stressing community rights, it also tilted the scale against the type of monopoly that would have hamstrung economic growth.

Taney, Ch. J., delivered the opinion of the court.—The questions involved in this case are of the gravest character, and the court have given to them the most anxious and deliberate consideration. The value of the right claimed by the plantiffs is large in amount; and many persons may, no doubt, be seriously affected in their pecuniary interests, by any decision which the court may pronounce; and the questions which have been raised as to the power of the several states, in relation to the corporations they have chartered, are pregnant with important consequences; not only to the individuals who are concerned in the corporate franchises, but to the communities in which they exist. The court are fully sensible, that it is their duty, in exercising the high powers conferred on them by the constitution of the United States, to deal with these great and extensive interests, with the utmost caution; guarding, so far as they have the power to do so, the rights of property, and at the same time, carefully abstaining from any encroachment on the rights reserved to the states. . . . [T]he object and end of all government is to promote the happiness and prosperity of the community by which it is established; and it can never be assumed, that the government intended to diminish its power of accomplishing the end for which it was

* 11 Peters 420, 535-53 (U.S. 1837).

created. And in a country like ours, free, active and enterprising, continually advancing in numbers and wealth, new channels of communication are daily found necessary, both for travel and trade, and are essential to the comfort, convenience and prosperity of the people. A state ought never to be presumed to surrender this power, because, like the taxing power, the whole community have an interest in preserving it undiminished. And when a corporation alleges, that a state has surrendered, for seventy years, its power of improvement and public accommodation, in a great and important line of travel, along which a vast number of its citizens must daily pass, the community have a right to insist, in the language of this court, above quoted, "that its abandonment ought not to be presumed, in a case, in which the deliberate purpose of the state to abandon it does not appear." The continued existence of a government would be of no great value, if, by implications and presumptions, it was disarmed of the powers necessary to accomplish the ends of its creation, and the functions it was designed to perform, transferred to the hands of privileged corporations. The rule of construction announced by the court, was not confined to the taxing power, nor is it so limited, in the opinion delivered. On the contrary, it was distinctly placed on the ground, that the interests of the community were concerned in preserving, undiminished, the power then in question; and whenever any power of the state is said to be surrendered or diminished, whether it be the taxing power, or any other affecting the public interest, the same principle applies, and the rule of construction must be the same. No one will question, that the interests of the great body of the people of the state, would, in this instance, be affected by the surrender of this great line of travel to a single corporation, with the right to exact toll, and exclude competition, for seventy years. While the rights of private property are sacredly guarded, we must not forget, that the community also have rights, and that the happiness and well-being of every citizen depends on their faithful preservation.

Adopting the rule of construction above stated as the settled one, we proceed to apply it to the charter of 1785, to the proprietors of the Charles River bridge. This act of incorporation is in the usual form, and the privileges such as are commonly given to corporations of that kind. It confers on them the ordinary faculties of a corporation, for the purpose of building the bridge; and establishes certain rates of toll, which the company are authorized to take: this is the whole grant. There is no exclusive privilege given to them over the waters of Charles river, above or below their bridge; no right to erect another bridge themselves, nor to prevent other persons from erecting one, no engagement from the state, that another shall not be erected; and no undertaking not to sanction competition, nor to make improvements that may diminish the amount of its income. Upon all these subjects, the charter is silent; and nothing is said in it about a line of travel, so much insisted on in the argument, in which they are to have exclusive privileges. No words are used, from which an intention to grant any of these rights can be inferred; if the plaintiff is entitled to them, it must be implied, simply, from the nature of the grant; and cannot be inferred, from the words by which the grant is made.

The relative position of the Warren bridge has already been described. It does not interrupt the passage over the Charles River bridge, nor make the way to it, or from it, less convenient. None of the faculties or franchises granted to that corporation, have been revoked by the legislature; and its right to take the tolls granted by the charter remains unaltered. In short, all the franchises and rights of property, enumerated in the charter, and there mentioned to have been granted to it, remain unimpaired. But its income is destroyed by the Warren bridge; which, being free, draws off the passengers and property which would have gone over it, and renders their franchise of no value. This is the gist of the complainant; for it is not pretended, that the erection of the Warren bridge would have done them any injury, or in any degree affected their right of property, if it had not diminished the amount of their tolls. In order, then, to entitle themselves to relief, it is necessary to show, that the legislature contracted not to do the act of which they complain; and that they impaired, or in other words, violated, that contract, by the erection of the Warren bridge.

The inquiry, then, is, does the charter contain such a contract on the part of the state? Is there any such stipulation to be found in that instrument? It must be admitted on all hands, that there is none; no words that even relate to another bridge, or to the diminution of their tolls, or to the line of travel. If a contract on that subject can be gathered from the charter, it must be by implication; and cannot be found in the words used. Can such an agreement be implied? The rule of construction before stated is an answer to the question: in charters of this description, no rights are taken from the public, or given to the corporation, beyond those which the words of the charter, by their natural and proper construction, purport to convey. There are no words which import such a contract as the plaintiffs in error contend for, and none can be implied; and the same answer must be given to them that was given by this court to Providence Bank. The whole community are interested in this inquiry, and they have a right to require that the power of promoting their comfort and convenience, and of advancing the public prosperity, by providing safe, convenient and cheap ways for the transportation of produce, and the purposes of travel, shall not be construed to have been surrendered or diminished by the state; unless it shall appear by plain words, that it was intended to be done. . . .

And what would be the fruits of this doctrine of implied contracts, on the part of the states, and of property in a line of travel, by a corporation, if it would now be sanctioned by this court? To what results would it lead us? If it is to be found in the charter to this bridge, the same process of reasoning must discover it, in the various acts which have been passed, within the last forty years, for turnpike companies. And what is to be the extent of the privileges of exclusion on the different sides of the road? The counsel who have so ably argued this case, have not attempted to define it by any certain boundaries. How far must the new improvement be distant from the old one? How near may you approach, without invading its rights in the privileged line? If this court should establish the principles now contended for, what is to become of the numerous railroads established on the same line of travel with turnpike companies; and which have rendered the franchises of the turnpike corporations of no value? Let it once be understood, that such charters carry with them these implied contracts, and give this unknown and undefined property in a line of travelling; and you will soon find the old turnpike corporations awakening from their sleep, and calling upon this court to put down the improvements which have taken their place. The millions of property which have been invested in railroads and canals, upon lines of travel which had been before occupied by turnpike corporations, will be put in jeopardy. We shall be thrown back to the improvements of the last century, and obliged to stand still, until the claims of the old turnpike corporations shall be satisfied; and they shall consent to permit these states to avail themselves of the lights of modern science, and to partake of the benefit of those improvements which are now adding to the wealth and prosperity, and the convenience and comfort, of every other part of the civilized world. Nor is this all. This court will find itself compelled to fix, by some arbitrary rule, the width of this new kind of property in a line of travel; for if such a right of property exists, we have no lights to guide us in marking out its extent, unless, indeed, we resort to the old feudal grants, and to the exclusive rights of ferries, by prescription, between towns; and are prepared to decide that when a turnpike road from one town to another, had been made, no railroad or canal, between these two points, could afterwards be established. This court are not prepared to sanction principles which must lead to such results.

Many other questions, of the deepest importance, have been raised and elaborately discussed in the argument. It is not necessary, for the decision of this case, to express our opinion upon them; and the court deem it proper to avoid volunteering an opinion on any question, involving the construction of the constitution, where the case itself does not bring the question directly before them, and make it their duty to decide upon it. Some questions, also, of a purely technical character, have been made and argued, as to the form of proceeding and the right to relief. But enough appears on the record, to bring out the great question in contest; and it is the interest of all parties concerned, that the real controversy should be settled, without further delay: and as the opinion of the court is pronounced on the main question in dispute here, and disposes of the whole case, it is altogether unnecessary to enter upon the examination of the forms of proceeding, in which the parties have brought it before the court.

The judgment of the supreme judicial court of the commonwealth of Massachusetts, dismissing the plaintiffs' bill, must, therefore, be affirmed, with costs.

READING NO. 9

Abraham Lincoln on the Court, 1858 and 1861*

The reaction to the Dred Scott decision and the wound it inflicted upon the Court are shown in these statements by Lincoln. The first is taken from Lincoln's reply in one of the Lincoln-Douglas debates, the second from Lincoln's First Inaugural Address. Both illustrate the refusal to be bound beyond the immediate case by Court decisions which are deemed incorrect—a view that has been asserted in opposition to the Court whenever its decisions have been opposed by sufficiently strong interests.

Then what is necessary for the nationalization of slavery? It is simply the next Dred Scott decision. It is merely for the Supreme Court to decide that no *State* under the Constitution can exclude it, just as they have already decided that under the Constitution neither Congress nor the Territorial Legislature can do it. When that is decided and acquiesced in, the whole thing is done. This being true, and this being the way as I think that slavery is to be made national, let us consider what Judge Douglas is doing every day to that end. In the first place, let us see what influence he is exerting on public sentiment. In this and like communities, public sentiment is everything. With public sentiment, nothing can fail; without it nothing can succeed. Consequently he who moulds public sentiment, goes deeper than he who enacts statutes or pronounces decisions. He makes statutes and decisions possible or impossible to be executed. This must be borne in mind, as also the additional fact that Judge Douglas is a man of vast influence, so great that it is enough for many

* *The Collected Works of Abraham Lincoln,* Vol. 3 (Basler ed., New Brunswick, 1953), pp. 27-29; J. D. Richardson, *A Compilation of the Messages and Papers of the Presidents,* Vol. 6 (Washington, 1897), pp. 9-10.

men to profess to believe anything, when they once find out that Judge Douglas professes to believe it. Consider also the attitude he occupies at the head of a large party—a party which he claims has a majority of all the voters in the country. This man sticks to a decision which forbids the people of a Territory from excluding slavery, and he does so not because he says it is right in itself—he does not give any opinion on that—but because it has been *decided by the court,* and being decided by the court, he is, and you are bound to take it in your political action as *law*—not that he judges at all of its merits, but because a decision of the court is to him a *"Thus saith the Lord."* [Applause.] He places it on that ground alone, and you will bear in mind that thus committing himself unreservedly to this decision, *commits him to the next one* just as firmly as to this. He did not commit himself on account of the merit or demerit of the decision, but it is a *Thus saith the Lord.* The next decision, as much as this, will be a *thus saith the Lord.* There is nothing that can divert or turn him away from this decision. It is nothing that I point out to him that his great prototype, Gen. Jackson, did not believe in the binding force of decisions. It is nothing to him that Jefferson did not so believe. I have said that I have often heard him approve of Jackson's course in disregarding the decision of the Supreme Court pronouncing a National Bank constitutional. He says, I did not hear him say so. He denies the accuracy of my recollection. I say he ought to know better than I, but I will make no question about this thing, though it still seems to me that I heard him say it twenty times. [Applause and laughter.] I will tell him though, that he now claims to stand on the Cincinnati platform, which affirms that Congress *cannot* charter a National Bank, in the teeth of that old standing decision that Congress *can* charter a bank. [Loud applause.] And I remind him of another piece of history on the question of respect for judicial decisions, and it is a piece of Illinois history, belonging to a time when the large party to which Judge Douglas belonged, were displeased with a decision of the Supreme Court of Illinois, because they had decided that a Governor could not remove a Secretary of State. You will find the whole story in Ford's History of Illinois, and I know that Judge Douglas will not deny that he was then in favor of overslaughing that decision by the mode of adding five new Judges, so as to vote down the four old ones. Not only so, but it ended in *the Judge's sitting down on that very bench as one of the five new Judges to break down the four old ones.* [Cheers and laughter.] It was in this way precisely that he got his title of Judge. Now, when the Judge tells me that men appointed conditionally to sit as members of a court, will have to be catechised beforehand upon some subject, I say "You know Judge; you have tried it." [Laughter.] When he says a court of this kind will lose the confidence of all men, will be prostituted and disgraced by such a proceeding, I say, "You know best, Judge; you have been through the mill." [Great laughter.] But I cannot shake Judge Douglas' teeth loose from the Dred Scott decision. Like some obstinate animal (I mean no disrespect,) that will hang on when he has once got his teeth fixed, you may cut off a leg, or you may tear away an arm, still he will not relax his hold. And so I may point out to the Judge, and say that he is bespattered all over, from the beginning of his political life to the present time, with attacks upon judicial decisions—I may cut off limb after limb of his public record, and strive to wrench him from a single dictum of the Court—yet I cannot divert him from it. He hangs to the last, to the Dred Scott decision. [Loud cheers.] These things show there is a purpose *strong as death and eternity* for which he adheres to this decision, and for which he will adhere to *all other decisions* of the same Court. [Vociferous applause.]

I do not forget the position assumed by some that constitutional questions are to be decided by the Supreme Court, nor do I deny that such decisions must be binding in any case upon the parties to a suit as to the object of that suit, while they are also entitled to very high respect and consideration in all parallel cases by all other departments of the Government. And while it is obviously possible that such decision may be erroneous in any given case, still the evil effect following it, being limited to that particular case, with the chance that it may be overruled and never become a precedent for other cases, can better be borne than could the evils of a different practice. At the same time, the candid citizen must confess that if the policy of the

Government upon vital questions affecting the whole people is to be irrevocably fixed by decisions of the Supreme Court, the instant they are made in ordinary litigation between parties in personal actions the people will have ceased to be their own rulers, having to that extent practically resigned their Government into the hands of that eminent tribunal. Nor is there in this view any assault upon the court or the judges. It is a duty from which they may not shrink to decide cases properly brought before them, and it is no fault of theirs if others seek to turn their decisions to political purposes.

READING NO. 10

Andrew Johnson's Veto of the McCardle Act, 1868*

Congress enacted in 1868 a law to bar the Supreme Court from hearing the appeal in the McCardle case because it feared a decision invalidating the Reconstruction Act. The statute in question was ultimately passed over President Johnson's veto, reprinted here. It strongly condemns the Congressional attack on the Court. Politically, of course, Johnson was unable to do more than protest. But his defense shows the opposition to Congressional supremacy over the Court, even in the heyday of the Radical Republicans.

Washington, D. C., *March 25, 1868.*
To the Senate of the United States:

I have considered, with such care as the pressure of other duties has permitted, a bill entitled "An act to amend an act entitled 'An act to amend the judiciary act, passed the 24th of September, 1789.'" Not being able to approve all of its provisions, I herewith return it to the Senate, in which House it originated, with a brief statement of my objections.

The first section of the bill meets my approbation, as, for the purpose of protecting the rights of property from the erroneous decision of inferior judicial tribunals, it provides means for obtaining uniformity, by appeal to the Supreme Court of the United States, in cases which have now become very numerous and of much public interest, and in which such remedy is not now allowed. The second section, however, takes away the right of appeal to that court in cases which involve the life and liberty of the citizen, and leaves them exposed to the judgment of numerous inferior tribunals. It is apparent that the two sections were conceived in a very different spirit, and I regret

---

* J. D. Richardson, *A Compilation of the Messages and Papers of the Presidents,* Vol. 6 (Washington, 1897), pp. 646-48.

that my objections to one impose upon me the necessity of withholding my sanction from the other.

I can not give my assent to a measure which proposes to deprive any person "restrained of his or her liberty in violation of the Constitution or of any treaty or law of the United States" from the right of appeal to the highest judicial authority known to our Government. To "secure the blessings of liberty to ourselves and our posterity" is one of the declared objects of the Federal Constitution. To assure these, guaranties are provided in the same instrument, as well against "unreasonable searches and seizures" as against the suspensions of "the privilege of the writ of *habeas corpus,* * * * unless when, in cases of rebellion or invasion, the public safety may require it." It was doubtless to afford the people the means of protecting and enforcing these inestimable privileges that the jurisdiction which this bill proposes to take away was conferred upon the Supreme Court of the nation. The act conferring that jurisdiction was approved on the 5th day of February, 1867, with a full knowledge of the motives that prompted its passage, and because it was believed to be necessary and right. Nothing has since occurred to disprove the wisdom and justness of the measures, and to modify it as now proposed would be to lessen the protection of the citizen from the exercise of arbitrary power and to weaken the safeguards of life and liberty, which can never be made too secure against illegal encroachments.

The bill not only prohibits the adjudication by the Supreme Court of cases in which appeals may hereafter be taken, but interdicts its jurisdiction on appeals which have already been made to that high judicial body. If, therefore, it should become a law, it will by its retroactive operation wrest from the citizen a remedy which he enjoyed at the time of his appeal. It will thus operate most harshly upon those who believe that justice has been denied them in the inferior courts.

The legislation proposed in the second section, it seems to me, is not in harmony with the spirit and intention of the Constitution. It can not fail to affect most injuriously the just equipoise of our system of Government, for it establishes a precedent which, if followed, may eventually sweep away every check on arbitrary and unconstitutional legislation. Thus far during the existence of the Government the Supreme Court of the United States has been viewed by the people as the true expounder of their Constitution, and in the most violent party conflicts its judgments and decrees have always been sought and deferred to with confidence and respect. In public estimation it combines judicial wisdom and impartiality in a greater degree than any other authority known to the Constitution, and any act which may be construed into or mistaken for an attempt to prevent or evade its decision on a question which affects the liberty of the citizens and agitates the country can not fail to be attended with unpropitious consequences. It will be justly held by a large portion of the people as an admission of the unconstitutionality of the act on which its judgment may be forbidden or forestalled, and may interfere with that willing acquiescence in its provisions which is necessary for the harmonious and efficient execution of any law.

For these reasons, thus briefly and imperfectly stated, and for others, of which want of time forbids the enumeration, I deem it my duty to withhold my assent from this bill, and to return it for the reconsideration of Congress.   ANDREW JOHNSON.

READING NO. 11

Allgeyer v. Louisiana, 1897*

This was the first case in which the Court expressly set aside a state law on the ground that it infringed upon substantive due process. The approach articulated by Justice Peckham was to be used with increasing frequency during the next forty years to restrict governmental authority, particularly in the area of economic regulation. Substantive due process and liberty of contract were to become serious hindrances to regulatory power. The law at issue in Allgeyer prohibited an individual from contracting with an out-of-state insurance company for the insurance of property within the state.

Mr. Justice Peckham . . . delivered the opinion of the court. . . .

The foregoing extracts have been made for the purpose of showing what general definitions have been given in regard to the meaning of the word "liberty" as used in the amendment, but we do not intend to hold that in no such case can the State exercise its police power. When and how far such power may be legitimately exercised with regard to these subjects must be left for determination to each case as it arises.

Has not a citizen of a State, under the provisions of the Federal Constitution above mentioned, a right to contract outside of the State for insurance on his property—a right of which state legislation cannot deprive him? We are not alluding to acts done within the State by an insurance company or its agents doing business therein, which are in violation of the state statutes. . . . When we speak of the liberty to contract for insurance or to do an act to effectuate such a contract already existing, we refer to and have in mind the facts of this case, where the contract was made outside the State, and as such was a valid and proper contract. The act done within the limits of

* 165 U.S. 578, 590-93 (1897).

the State under the circumstances of this case and for the purpose therein mentioned, we hold a proper act, one which the defendants were at liberty to perform and which the state legislature had no right to prevent, at least with reference to the Federal Constitution. To deprive the citizen of such a right as herein described without due process of law is illegal. Such a statute as this in question is not due process of law, because it prohibits an act which under the Federal Constitution the defendants had a right to perform. This does not interfere in any way with the acknowledged right of the State to enact such legislation in the legitimate exercise of its police or other powers as to it may seem proper. In the exercise of such right, however, care must be taken not to infringe upon those other rights of the citizen which are protected by the Federal Constitution.

In the privilege of pursuing an ordinary calling or trade and of acquiring, holding and selling property must be embraced the right to make all proper contracts in relation thereto, and although it may be conceded that this right to contract in relation to persons or property or to do business within the jurisdiction of the State may be regulated and sometimes prohibited when the contracts or business conflict with the policy of the State as contained in its statutes, yet the power does not and cannot extend to prohibiting a citizen from making contracts of the nature involved in this case outside of the limits and jurisdiction of the State, and which are also to be performed outside of such jurisdiction. . . .

The Atlantic Mutual Insurance Company of New York has done no business of insurance within the State of Louisiana and has not subjected itself to any provisions of the statute in question. It had the right to enter into a contract in New York with citizens of Louisiana for the purpose of insuring the property of its citizens, even if that property were in the State of Louisiana, and correlatively the citizens of Louisiana had the right without the State of entering into contract with an insurance company for the same purpose. Any act of the state legislature which should prevent the entering into such a contract, or the mailing within the State of Louisiana of such a notification as is mentioned in this case, is an improper and illegal interference with the conduct of the citizen, although residing in Louisiana, in his right to contract and to carry out the terms of a contract validly entered into outside and beyond the jurisdiction of the State. . . .

For these reasons we think the statute in question, No. 66 of the Laws of Louisiana of 1894, was a violation of the Federal Constitution, and afforded no justification for the judgment awarded by that court against the plaintiffs in error. That judgment must, therefore, be

> *Reversed, and the case remanded to the Supreme Court of Louisiana for further proceedings not inconsistent with this opinion.*

READING NO. 12

Mr. Dooley on the Court, 1901*

Few comments on the Court have been quoted more frequently than Mr. Dooley's "th' Supreme Coort follows th' iliction returns." It is not generally realized that this comment was made in an acute analysis of the decision in the 1901 Insular Cases. The Court's performance there was one of its poorest, with a proliferation of opinions (of the type usually associated with more recent Courts), characterized by a literary style that can charitably be termed inelegant. The Dooley parody is a wonderful reflection of the puzzlement of the layman in the face of much high-bench action. Mr. Dooley himself was, of course, the creation of humorist Finley Peter Dunne.

"I see," said Mr. Dooley, "Th' supreme coort has decided th' constitution don't follow th' flag."

"Who said it did?" asked Mr. Hennessy.

"Some wan," said Mr. Dooley. "It happened a long time ago an' I don't raymimber clearly how it come up, but some fellow said that ivrywhere th' constitution wint, th' flag was sure to go. 'I don't believe wan wurrud iv it,' says th' other fellow. 'Ye can't make me think th' constitution is goin' thrapezin' around ivrywhere a young liftnant in th' ar-rmy takes it into his head to stick a flag pole. It's too old. It's a home-stayin' constitution with a blue coat with brass buttons onto it, an' it walks with a goold-headed cane. It's old an' it's feeble an' it prefers to set on th' front stoop an' amuse th' childher. It wudden't last a minyit in thim thropical climes. 'T wud get a pain in th' fourteenth amindmint an' die befure th' doctors cud get ar-round to cut it out. No, sir, we'll keep it with us, an' threat it tenderly without too much hard wurruk, an' whin it plays out entirely we'll give it dacint buryal an' incorp'rate oursilves under th' laws iv Noo

* *Mr. Dooley on the Choice of Law* (Bander, ed., Charlottesville, 1963), pp. 47-52.

Jarsay. That's what we'll do,' says he. 'But,' says th' other, 'if it wants to thravel, why not lave it?' 'But it don't want to.' 'I say it does.' 'How'll we find out?' 'We'll ask th' supreme coort. They'll know what's good f'r it.' "

"So it wint up to th' supreme coort. They'se wan thing about th' supreme coort, if ye lave annything to thim, ye lave it to thim. Ye don't get a check that entitles ye to call f'r it in an hour. The supreme coort iv th' United States ain't in anny hurry about catchin' th' mails. It don't have to make th' las' car. I'd back th' Aujitoroom again it anny day f'r a foot race. If ye're lookin' f'r a game iv quick decisions an' base hits, ye've got to hire another empire. It niver gives a decision till th' crowd has dispersed an' th' players have packed their bats in th' bags an' started f'r home.

"F'r awhile ivrybody watched to see what th' supreme coort wud do. I knew mesilf I felt I cudden't make another move in th' game till I heerd fr'm thim. Buildin' op'rations was suspinded an' we sthud wringin' our hands outside th' dure waitin' f'r information fr'm th' bedside. 'What're they doin' now?' 'They just put th' argymints iv larned counsel in th' ice box an' th' chief justice is in a corner writin' a pome. Brown J. an' Harlan J. is discussin' th' condition iv th' Roman Empire befure th' fire. Th' rest iv th' coort is considherin' th' question iv whether they ought or ought not to wear ruchin' on their skirts an' hopin' crinoline won't come in again. No decision to-day?' An' so it wint f'r days, an' weeks an' months. Th' men that had argyied that th' constitution ought to shadow th' flag to all th' tough resorts on th' Passyfic coast an' th' men that argyied that th' flag was so lively that no constitution cud follow it an' survive, they died or lost their jobs or wint back to Salem an' were f'rgotten. Expansionists contracted an' anti-expansionists blew up an' little childher was born into th' wurruld an' grew to manhood an' niver heerd iv Porther Ricky except whin some wan get a job there. I'd about made up me mind to thry an' put th' thing out iv me thoughts an' go back to wurruk when I woke up wan mornin' an' see be th' pa-aper that th' Supreme Coort had warned th' constitution to lave th' flag alone an' tind to its own business.

"That's what th' pa-aper says, but I've r-read over th' decision an' I don't see annything iv th' kind there. They'se not a wurrud about th' flag an' not enough to tire ye about th' constitution. 'T is a matther iv limons, Hinnissy, that th' Supreme Coort has been settin' on f'r this gineration—a cargo iv limons sint fr'm Porther Ricky to some Eyetalian in Philydelphy. Th' decision was r-read be Brown J., him bein' th' las' justice to make up his mind, an' ex-officio, as Hogan says, th' first to speak, after a crool an' bitther contest. Says Brown J: 'Th' question here is wan iv such gr-reat importance that we've been sthrugglin' over it iver since ye see us las' an' on'y come to a decision (Fuller C.J., Gray J., Harlan J., Shiras J., McKenna J., White J., Brewer J., an' Peckham J. dissentin' fr'm me an' each other) because iv th' hot weather comin' on. Wash'n'ton is a dhreadful place in summer (Fuller C.J. dissentin'). Th' whole fabric iv our government is threatened, th' lives iv our people an' th' progress iv civilization put to th' bad. Men are excited. But why? We ar-re not. (Harlan J., "I am." Fuller C.J. dissentin', but not f'r th' same reason.) This thing must be settled wan way or th' other undher that dear ol' constitution be varchue iv which we are here an' ye ar-re there an' Congress is out West practicin' law. Now what does th' constitution say? We'll look it up thoroughly whin we get through with this case (th' rest iv th' coort dissentin'). In th' manetime we must be governed be th' ordnances iv th' Khan iv Beloochistan, th' laws iv Hinnery th' Eighth, th' opinyon iv Justice iv th' Peace Oscar Larson in th' case iv th' township iv Red Wing versus Petersen, an' th' Dhred Scott decision. What do they say about limons? Nawthin' at all. Again we take th' Dhred Scott decision. This is wan iv th' worst I iver r-read. If I cudden't write a betther wan with blindhers on, I'd leap off th' bench. This horrible fluke iv a decision throws a gr-reat, an almost dazzlin' light on th' case. I will turn it off. (McKenna J. concurs, but thinks it ought to be blowed out.) But where was I? I must put on me specs. Oh, about th' limons. Well, th' decision iv th' Coort (th' others dissentin') is as follows: First, that th' Disthrict iv Columbya is a state; second, that it is not; third, that New York is a state; fourth, that it is a crown colony; fifth, that all states ar-re states an' all territories ar-re territories in th' eyes iv other powers, but Gawd knows what they ar-re at home. In th' case iv Hogan versus Mullins, th' decision is he must paper th' barn. (Hinnery VIII, sixteen, six, four, eleven.) In Wiggins varsus et al. th' cow belonged. (Louis XIV, 90 in rem.) In E. P. Vigore varsus Ad Lib., the custody iv th' childher. I'll now fall back a furlong or two in me chair, while me larned but misguided collagues r-read th' Histhry iv Iceland to show ye how wrong I am. But mind ye, what I've said goes. I let thim talk because it exercises their throats, but ye've heard all th' decision on this limon case that'll get into th' fourth reader.' A voice fr'm th' audjeence, 'Do I get me money back?' Brown J.: 'Who ar-re ye?' Th' Voice: 'Th' man that ownded th' limons.' Brown J.: 'I don't know.' (Gray J., White J., dissentin' an' th' r-rest iv th' birds concurrin' but f'r entirely diff'rent reasons.)

"An' there ye have th' decision, Hinnissy, that's shaken th' intellicts iv th' nation to their very foundations, or will if they thry to read it. 'Tis all r-right. Look it over some time. 'T is fine spoort if ye don't care f'r checkers. Some say it laves th' flag up in th' air an' some say that's where it laves th' constitution. Annyhow, somethin's in th' air. But there's wan thing I'm sure about."

"What's that?" asked Mr. Hennessy.

"That is," said Mr. Dooley, "no matther whether th' constitution follows th' flag or not, th' supreme coort follows th' iliction returns."

READING NO. 13

Justice Holmes, Dissenting, 1905 and 1930*

Substantive due process was used by the Court from 1897 to 1937 to restrict governmental efforts to curb economic excesses. The Court's tendency during this period to equate the Constitution with the requirements of laissez-faire called forth the vigorous dissents of Justices Holmes and Brandeis. These are two of the most famous Holmes dissents. The first was delivered in Lochner v. New York *(1905), the second in* Baldwin v. Missouri *(1930). Both are good illustrations of the qualities that made Holmes the most famous dissenter in Supreme Court history.*

A.

MR. JUSTICE HOLMES dissenting.

I regret sincerely that I am unable to agree with the judgment in this case, and that I think it my duty to express my dissent.

This case is decided upon an economic theory which a large part of the country does not entertain. If it were a question whether I agreed with that theory, I should desire to study it further and long before making up my mind. But I do not conceive that to be my duty, because I strongly believe that my agreement or disagreement has nothing to do with the right of a majority to embody their opinions in law. It is settled by various decisions of this court that state constitutions and state laws may regulate life in many ways which we as legislators might think as injudicious or if you like as tyrannical as this, and which equally with this interfere with the liberty to contract. Sunday laws and usury laws are ancient examples. A more modern one is the prohibition of lotteries. The liberty of the

* 198 U.S. 45, 75-76 (1905); 281 U.S. 586, 595-96 (1930).

citizen to do as he likes so long as he does not interfere with the liberty of others to do the same, which has been a shibboleth for some well-known writers, is interfered with by school laws, by the Post Office, by every state or municipal institution which takes his money for purposes thought desirable, whether he likes it or not. The Fourteenth Amendment does not enact Mr. Herbert Spencer's Social Statics. The other day we sustained the Massachusetts vaccination law. *Jacobson* v. *Massachusetts*, 197 U. S. 11. United States and state statutes and decisions cutting down the liberty to contract by way of combination are familiar to this court. *Northern Securities Co.* v. *United States*, 193 U. S. 197. Two years ago we upheld the prohibition of sales of stock on margins or for future delivery in the constitution of California. *Otis* v. *Parker,* 187 U. S. 606. The decision sustaining an eight hour law for miners is still recent. *Holden* v. *Hardy,* 169 U. S. 366. Some of these laws embody convictions or prejudices which judges are likely to share. Some may not. But a constitution is not intended to embody a particular economic theory, whether of paternalism and the organic relation of the citizen to the State or of *laissez faire*. It is made for people of fundamentally differing views, and the accident of our finding certain opinions natural and familiar or novel and even shocking ought not to conclude our judgment upon the question whether statutes embodying them conflict with the Constitution of the United States.

General propositions do not decide concrete cases. The decision will depend on a judgment or intuition more subtle than any articulate major premise. But I think that the proposition just stated, if it is accepted, will carry us far toward the end. Every opinion tends to become a law. I think that the word liberty in the Fourteenth Amendment is perverted when it is held to prevent the natural outcome of a dominant opinion, unless it can be said that a rational and fair man necessarily would admit that the statute proposed would infringe fundamental principles as they have been understood by the traditions of our people and our law. It does not need research to show that no such sweeping condemnation can be passed upon the statute before us. A reasonable man might think it a proper measure on the score of health. Men whom I certainly could not pronounce unreasonable would uphold it as a first instalment of a general regulation of the hours of work. Whether in the latter aspect it would be open to the charge of inequality I think it unnecessary to discuss.

B.

MR. JUSTICE HOLMES.

Although this decision hardly can be called a surprise after *Farmers Loan & Trust Co.* v. *Minnesota,* 280 U. S. 204 and *Safe Deposit & Trust Co.* v. *Virginia,* 280 U. S. 83, and although I stated my views in those cases, still, as the term is not over, I think it legitimate to add one or two reflections to what I have said before. I have not yet adequately expressed the more than anxiety that I feel at the ever increasing scope given to the Fourteenth Amendment in cutting down what I believe to be the constitutional rights of the States. As the decisions now stand, I see hardly any limit but the sky to the invalidating of those rights if they happen to strike a majority of this Court as for any reason undesirable. I cannot believe that the Amendment was intended to give us *carte blanche* to embody our economic or moral beliefs in its prohibitions. Yet I can think of no narrower reason that seems to me to justify the present and the earlier decisions to which I have referred. Of course the words "due process of law," if taken in their literal meaning, have no application to this case; and while it is too late to deny that they have been given a much more extended and artificial signification, still we ought to remember the great caution shown by the Constitution in limiting the power of the States, and should be slow to construe the clause in the Fourteenth Amendment as committing to the Court, with no guide but the Court's own discretion, the validity of whatever laws the States may pass. In this case the bonds, notes and bank accounts were within the power and received the protection of the State of Missouri; the notes, so far as appears, were within the considerations that I offered in the earlier decisions mentioned, so that logically Missouri was justified in demanding a *quid pro quo;* the practice of taxation in such circumstances I think has been ancient and widespread, and the tax was warranted by decisions of this

Court. *Liverpool & London & Globe Ins. Co.* v. *Assessors for the Parish of Orleans,* 221 U. S. 346, 354, 355. *Wheeler* v. *Sohmer,* 233 U. S. 434. (I suppose that these cases and many others now join *Blackstone* v. *Miller* on the *Index Expurgatorius*—but we need an authoritative list.) It seems to me to be exceeding our powers to declare such a tax a denial of due process of law.

And what are the grounds? Simply, so far as I can see, that it is disagreeable to a bondowner to be taxed in two places. Very probably it might be good policy to restrict taxation to a single place, and perhaps the technical conception of domicil may be the best determinant. But it seems to me that if that result is to be reached it should be reached through understanding among the States, by uniform legislation or otherwise, not by evoking a constitutional prohibition from the void of 'due process of law,' when logic, tradition and authority have united to declare the right of the State to lay the now prohibited tax.

READING NO. 14

F.D.R. on Court-Packing, March 9, 1937*

The Supreme Court decisions invalidating much of the early New Deal program led directly to President Roosevelt's plan early in 1937 to reorganize the judiciary. In practical effect, the F.D.R. plan would have given the President the power to pack the Supreme Court by giving him authority to appoint a new justice for every incumbent over seventy who failed to retire. In this "fireside chat," F.D.R. sought to rally public support for his plan.

Last Thursday I described in detail certain economic problems which everyone admits now face the Nation. For the many messages which have come to me after that speech, and which it is physically impossible to answer individually, I take this means of saying "thank you."

Tonight, sitting at my desk in the White House, I make my first radio report to the people in my second term of office. . . .

The American people have learned from the depression. For in the last three national elections an overwhelming majority of them voted a mandate that the Congress and the President begin the task of providing that protection—not after long years of debate, but now.

The Courts, however, have cast doubts on the ability of the elected Congress to protect us against catastrophe by meeting squarely our modern social and economic conditions.

We are at a crisis in our ability to proceed with that protection. It is a quiet crisis. There are no lines of depositors outside closed banks. But to the far-sighted it is far-reaching in its possibilities of injury to America.

I want to talk with you very simply about the need for present action in this crisis—the need to meet the unanswered challenge of one-third of a Nation ill-nourished, ill-clad, ill-housed.

* *The Public Papers and Addresses of Franklin D. Roosevelt,* 1937 Volume (Rosenman ed., New York, 1941), pp. 122-33.

Last Thursday I described the American form of Government as a three horse team provided by the Constitution to the American people so that their field might be plowed. The three horses are, of course, the three branches of government—the Congress, the Executive and the Courts. Two of the horses are pulling in unison today; the third is not. Those who have intimated that the President of the United States is trying to drive that team, overlook the simple fact that the President, as Chief Executive, is himself one of the three horses.

It is the American people themselves who are in the driver's seat.

It is the American people themselves who want the furrow plowed.

It is the American people themselves who expect the third horse to pull in unison with the other two. . . .

. . . [S]ince the rise of the modern movement for social and economic progress through legislation, the Court has more and more often and more and more boldly asserted a power to veto laws passed by the Congress and State Legislatures in complete disregard of this original limitation.

In the last four years the sound rule of giving statutes the benefit of all reasonable doubt has been cast aside. The Court has been acting not as a judicial body, but as a policy-making body.

When the Congress has sought to stabilize national agriculture, to improve the conditions of labor, to safeguard business against unfair competition, to protect our national resources, and in many other ways, to serve our clearly national needs, the majority of the Court has been assuming the power to pass on the wisdom of these Acts of the Congress—and to approve or disapprove the public policy written into these laws. . . .

The Court in addition to the proper use of its judicial functions has improperly set itself up as a third House of the Congress—a super-legislature, as one of the justices has called it—reading into the Constitution words and implications which are not there, and which were never intended to be there.

We have, therefore, reached the point as a Nation where we must take action to save the Constitution from the Court and the Court from itself. We must find a way to take an appeal from the Supreme Court to the Constitution itself. We want a

Supreme Court which will do justice under the Constitution—not over it. In our Courts we want a government of laws and not of men.

I want—as all Americans want—an independent judiciary as proposed by the framers of the Constitution. That means a Supreme Court that will enforce the Constitution as written—that will refuse to amend the Constitution by the arbitrary exercise of judicial power—amendment by judicial say-so. It does not mean a judiciary so independent that it can deny the existence of facts universally recognized. . . .

When I commenced to review the situation with the problem squarely before me, I came by a process of elimination to the conclusion that, short of amendments, the only method which was clearly constitutional, and would at the same time carry out other much needed reforms, was to infuse new blood into all our Courts. We must have men worthy and equipped to carry out impartial justice. But, at the same time, we must have Judges who will bring to the Courts a present-day sense of the Constitution—Judges who will retain in the Courts the judicial functions of a court, and reject the legislative powers which the courts have today assumed. . . .

What is my proposal? It is simply this: whenever a Judge or Justice of any Federal Court has reached the age of seventy and does not avail himself of the opportunity to retire on a pension, a new member shall be appointed by the President then in office, with the approval, as required by the Constitution, of the Senate of the United States.

That plan has two chief purposes. By bringing into the judicial system a steady and continuing stream of new and younger blood, I hope, first, to make the administration of all Federal justice speedier and, therefore, less costly; secondly, to bring to the decision of social and economic problems younger men who have had personal experience and contact with modern facts and circumstances under which average men have to live and work. This plan will save our national Constitution from hardening of the judicial arteries.

The number of Judges to be appointed would depend wholly on the decision of present Judges now over seventy, or those who would subsequently reach the age of seventy.

If, for instance, any one of the six Justices of the Supreme Court now over the age of seventy should retire as provided under the plan, no additional place would be created. Consequently, although there never can be more than fifteen, there may be only fourteen, or thirteen, or twelve. And there may be only nine.

There is nothing novel or radical about this idea. It seeks to maintain the Federal bench in full vigor. . . .

Those opposing this plan have sought to arouse prejudice and fear by crying that I am seeking to "pack" the Supreme Court and that a baneful precedent will be established.

What do they mean by the words "packing the Court"?

Let me answer this question with a bluntness that will end all *honest* misunderstanding of my purposes.

If by that phrase "packing the Court" it is charged that I wish to place on the bench spineless puppets who would disregard the law and would decide specific cases as I wished them to be decided; I make this answer: that no President fit for his office would appoint, and no Senate of honorable men fit for their office would confirm, that kind of appointees to the Supreme Court.

But if by that phrase the charge is made that I would appoint and the Senate would confirm Justices worthy to sit beside present members of the Court who understand those modern conditions, that I will appoint Justices who will not undertake to override the judgment of the Congress on legislative policy, that I will appoint Justices who will act as Justices and not as legislators—if the appointment of such Justices can be called "packing the Courts," then I say that I and with me the vast majority of the American people favor doing just that thing—now. . . .

I now propose that we establish by law an assurance against any such ill-balanced Court in the future. I propose that hereafter, when a Judge reaches the age of seventy, a new and younger Judge shall be added to the Court automatically. In this way I propose to enforce a sound public policy by law instead of leaving the composition of our Federal Courts, including the highest, to be determined by chance or the personal decision of individuals.

If such a law as I propose is regarded as establishing a new precedent, is it not a most desirable precedent?

Like all lawyers, like all Americans, I regret the necessity of this controversy. But the welfare of the United States, and indeed of the Constitution itself, is what we all must think about first. Our difficulty with the Court today rises not from the Court as an institution but from human beings within it. But we cannot yield our constitutional destiny to the personal judgment of a few men who, being fearful of the future, would deny us the necessary means of dealing with the present.

This plan of mine is no attack on the Court; it seeks to restore the Court to its rightful and historic place in our system of Constitutional Government and to have it resume its high task of building anew on the Constitution "a system of living law." . . .

Two groups oppose my plan on the ground that they favor a constitutional amendment. The first includes those who fundamentally object to social and economic legislation along modern lines. This is the same group who during the campaign last Fall tried to block the mandate of the people.

Now they are making a last stand. And the strategy of that last order to kill off by delay the legislation demanded by the mandate.

To them I say: I do not think you will be able long to fool the American people as to your purposes.

The other group is composed of those who honestly believe the amendment process is the best and who would be willing to support a reasonable amendment if they could agree on one.

To them I say: we cannot rely on an amendment as the immediate or only answer to our present difficulties. When the time comes for action, you will find that many of those who pretend to support you will sabotage any constructive amendment which is proposed. Look at these strange bed-fellows of yours. When before have you found them really at your side in your fights for progress?

And remember one thing more. Even if an amendment were passed, and even if in the years to come it were to be ratified, its meaning would depend upon the kind of Justices who would be sitting on the Supreme Court bench. An amendment, like the

Tutoring Notes
Academic Success Center

Student: Carlos Rovere

Date: 11-21-05

Course #: EAP 0460

Instructor: Valerie

What We Did:
- ☐ HW
- ☐ Test Prep

Talked about ASC resources
Advise about visiting counseling

Future Goals:
- ☒ Return
- ☐ See Instructor

Tutor: _____

White: Instructor   Yellow: ASC   Pink: Student

rest of the Constitution, is what the Justices say it is rather than what its framers or you might hope it is.

This proposal of mine will not infringe in the slightest upon the civil or religious liberties so dear to every American.

My record as Governor and as President proves my devotion to those liberties. You who know me can have no fear that I would tolerate the destruction by any branch of government of any part of our heritage of freedom.

The present attempt by those opposed to progress to play upon the fears of danger to personal liberty brings again to mind that crude and cruel strategy tried by the same opposition to frighten the workers of America in a pay-envelope propaganda against the Social Security Law. The workers were not fooled by that propaganda then. The people of America will not be fooled by such propaganda now.

I am in favor of action through legislation:

First, because I believe that it can be passed at this session of the Congress.

Second, because it will provide a reinvigorated, liberal-minded Judiciary necessary to furnish quicker and cheaper justice from bottom to top.

Third, because it will provide a series of Federal Courts willing to enforce the Constitution as written, and unwilling to assert legislative powers by writing into it their own political and economic policies.

During the past half century the balance of power between the three great branches of the Federal Government, has been tipped out of balance by the Courts in direct contradiction of the high purposes of the framers of the Constitution. It is my purpose to restore that balance. You who know me will accept my solemn assurance that in a world in which democracy is under attack, I seek to make American democracy succeed. You and I will do our part.

READING NO. 15

Chief Justice Hughes in Defense of the Court, March 21, 1937*

The F.D.R. Court-packing plan generated bitter opposition throughout the country and was ultimately rejected in a strong report of the Senate Judiciary Committee, which termed the plan "an invasion of judicial power such as has never before been attempted in this country." An important factor in rallying resistance to the F.D.R. plan was this letter of Chief Justice Hughes, which showed plainly the weakness of the President's ostensible purpose of dealing with an over-age Court unable to cope with its docket.

Chief Justice of the United States.
Washington, D. C., March 21, 1937.

Hon. Burton K. Wheeler,
   United States Senate, Washington, D. C.

My Dear Senator Wheeler: In response to your inquiries, I have the honor to present the following statement with respect to the work of the Supreme Court:

1. The Supreme Court is fully abreast of its work. When we rose on March 15 (for the present recess) we had heard argument in cases in which certiorari had been granted only 4 weeks before—February 15.

During the current term, which began last October and which we call "October term, 1936", we have heard argument on the merits in 150 cases (180 numbers) and we have 28 cases (30 numbers) awaiting argument. We shall be able to hear all these cases, and such others as may come up for argument, before our adjournment for the term. There is no congestion of cases upon our calendar.

* Senate Report 711, 75th Cong., 1st Sess. (Washington, 1937), pp. 38-40.

JUSTICE HUGHES IN DEFENSE OF THE COURT 147

This gratifying condition has obtained for several years. We have been able for several terms to adjourn after disposing of all cases which are ready to be heard. . . .

During the present term we have thus far disposed of 666 cases which include petitions for certiorari and cases which have been argued on the merits and already decided. . . .

I should add that petitions of certiorari are not apportioned among the Justices. In all matters before the Court, except in the more routine of administration, all the Justices—unless for some reason a Justice is disqualified or unable to act in a particular case—participate in the decision. This applies to the grant or refusal of petitions for certiorari. Furthermore, petitions for certiorari are granted if four Justices think they should be. A vote by a majority is not required in such cases. Even if two or three of the Justices are strongly of the opinion that certiorari should be allowed, frequently the other Justices will acquiesce in their view, but the petition is always granted if four so vote

6. The work of passing upon these applications for certiorari is laborious but the Court is able to perform it adequately. Observations have been made as to the vast number of pages of records and briefs that are submitted in the course of a term. The total is imposing but the suggested conclusion is hasty and rests on an illusory basis. Records are replete with testimony and evidence of facts. But the questions on certiorari are questions of law. So many cases turn on the facts, principles of law not being in controversy. It is only when the facts are interwoven with the questions of law which we should review that the evidence must be examined and then only to the extent that it is necessary to decide the questions of law.

This at once disposes of a vast number of factual controversies where the parties have been fully heard in the courts below and have no right to burden the Supreme Court with the dispute which interests no one but themselves.

This is also true of controversies over contracts and documents of all sorts which involve only questions of concern to the immediate parties. The applicant for certiorari is required to state in his petition the grounds for his application and in a host of cases that disclosure itself disposes of his request. So that the number of pages of records and briefs afford no satisfactory criterion of the actual work involved. It must also be remembered that Justices who have been dealing with such matters for years have the aid of a long and varied experience in separating the chaff from the wheat.

I think that it is safe to say that about 60 percent of the applications for certiorari are wholly without merit and ought never to have been made. There are probably about 20 percent or so in addition which have a fair degree of plausability but which fail to survive critical examination. The remainder, falling short, I believe, of 20 percent, show substantial grounds and are granted. I think that it is the view of the members of the Court that if any error is made in dealing with these applications it is on the side of liberality.

7. An increase in the number of Justices of the Supreme Court, apart from any question of policy, which I do not discuss, would not promote the efficiency of the Court. It is believed that it would impair that efficiency so long as the Court acts as a unit. There would be more judges to hear, more judges to confer, more judges to discuss, more judges to be convinced and to decide. The present number of Justices is thought to be large enough so far as the prompt, adequate, and efficient conduct of the work of the Court is concerned. As I have said, I do not speak of any other considerations in view of the appropriate attitude of the Court in relation to questions of policy.

I understand that it has been suggested that with more Justices the Court could hear cases in divisions. It is believed that such a plan would be impracticable. A large proportion of the cases we hear are important and a decision by a part of the Court would be unsatisfactory.

I may also call attention to the provisions of article III, section 1, of the Constitution that the judicial power of the United States shall be vested "in one Supreme Court" and in such inferior courts as the Congress may from time to time ordain and establish. The Constitution does not appear to authorize two or more Supreme Courts or two or more parts of a supreme court functioning in effect as separate courts.

On account of the shortness of time I have not been able to consult with the members of the Court generally with respect to the foregoing statement, but I am confident that it is in accord with the views of the Justices. I should say, however, that I have been able to consult with Mr. Justice Van Devanter and Mr. Justice Brandeis, and I am at liberty to say that the statement is approved by them.

I have the honor to remain,
    Respectfully yours,

                      CHARLES E. HUGHES,
                 Chief Justice of the United States.

READING NO. 16

Griffin v. Illinois, 1956*

This case well illustrates one of the primary concerns of the present Court—to ensure equality in the field of criminal justice. The opinion here has served as a catalyst in focusing attention on the problems of the poor in securing equal justice and has been the foundation for more recent decisions expanding the egalitarian concept in different areas of the law. The language is typical of the Warren Court in its broad approach to the immediate issue presented.

MR. JUSTICE BLACK announced the judgment of the Court. . . .

Illinois law provides that "Writs of error in all criminal cases are writs of right and shall be issued of course." The question presented here is whether Illinois may, consistent with the Due Process and Equal Protection Clauses of the Fourteenth Amendment, administer this statute so as to deny adequate appellate review to the poor while granting such review to all others.

The petitioners Griffin and Crenshaw were tried together and convicted of armed robbery in the Criminal Court of Cook County, Illinois. Immediately after their conviction they filed a motion in the trial court asking that a certified copy of the entire record, including a stenographic transcript of the proceedings, be furnished them without cost. They alleged that they were "poor persons with no means of paying the necessary fees to acquire the Transcript and Court Records needed to prosecute an appeal. . . ." These allegations were not denied. . . .

Counsel for Illinois concedes that these petitioners needed a transcript in order to get adequate appellate review of their alleged trial errors. There is no contention that petitioners were dilatory in their efforts to get appellate review, or that the Illinois Supreme Court denied review on the ground that the alle-

* 351 U.S. 12, 13-20 (1956).

gations of trial error were insufficient. We must therefore assume for purposes of this decision that errors were committed in the trial which would merit reversal, but that the petitioners could not get appellate review of those errors solely because they were too poor to buy a stenographic transcript. Counsel for Illinois denies that this violates either the Due Process or the Equal Protection Clause. . . .

Providing equal justice for poor and rich, weak and powerful alike is an age-old problem. People have never ceased to hope and strive to move closer to that goal. This hope, at least in part, brought about in 1215 the royal concessions of Magna Charta: "To no one will we sell, to no one will we refuse, or delay, right or justice. . . . No free man shall be taken or imprisoned, or disseised, or outlawed, or exiled, or anywise destroyed; nor shall we go upon him nor send upon him, but by the lawful judgment of his peers or by the law of the land." These pledges were unquestionably steps toward a fairer and more nearly equal application of criminal justice. In this tradition, our own constitutional guaranties of due process and equal protection both call for procedures in criminal trials which allow no invidious discriminations between persons and different groups of persons. Both equal protection and due process emphasize the central aim of our entire judicial system—all people charged with crime must, so far as the law is concerned, "stand on an equality before the bar of justice in every American court." *Chambers* v. *Florida,* 309 U. S. 227, 241. See also *Yick Wo* v. *Hopkins,* 118 U. S. 356, 369.

Surely no one would contend that either a State or the Federal Government could constitutionally provide that defendants unable to pay court costs in advance should be denied the right to plead not guilty or to defend themselves in court. Such a law would make the constitutional promise of a fair trial a worthless thing. Notice, the right to be heard, and the right to counsel would under such circumstances be meaningless promises to the poor. In criminal trials a State can no more discriminate on account of poverty than on account of religion, race, or color. Plainly the ability to pay costs in advance bears no rational relationship to a defendant's guilt or innocence and could not be used as an excuse to deprive a defendant of a fair trial. Indeed, a provision in the Constitution of Illinois of 1818 provided that every person in Illinois "ought to obtain right and justice freely, and without being obliged to purchase it, completely and without denial, promptly and without delay, conformably to the laws."

There is no meaningful distinction between a rule which would deny the poor the right to defend themselves in a trial court and one which effectively denies the poor an adequate appellate review accorded to all who have money enough to pay the costs in advance. It is true that a State is not required by the Federal Constitution to provide appellate courts or a right to appellate review at all. See, *e. g., McKane* v. *Durston,* 153 U. S. 684, 687-688. But that is not to say that a State that does grant appellate review can do so in a way that discriminates against some convicted defendants on account of their poverty. Appellate review has now become an integral part of the Illinois trial system for finally adjudicating the guilt or innocence of a defendant. Consequently at all stages of the proceedings the Due Process and Equal Protection Clauses protect persons like petitioners from invidious discriminations. . . .

Such a denial is a misfit in a country dedicated to affording equal justice to all and special privileges to none in the administration of its criminal law. There can be no equal justice where the kind of trial a man gets depends on the amount of money he has. Destitute defendants must be afforded as adequate appellate review as defendants who have money enough to buy transcripts. . . .

The judgment of the Supreme Court of Illinois is vacated and the cause is remanded to that court. . . .

READING NO. 17

Georgia Interposition Resolution, 1956*

After the Supreme Court's 1954 decision outlawing school segregation, so-called interposition resolutions were adopted by the legislature of several Southern states, of which this Georgia one is typical. They revive the doctrine first enunciated in the Virginia Resolutions drafted by Madison in 1798 and later relied on by Southern statesmen such as Calhoun. From a legal point of view, the interposition doctrine is no more sound today than it was in Calhoun's day. Its resurrection is, in many ways, more interesting to students of psychology than to students of constitutional law.

House Resolution No. 185 of the 1956 Session
of the General Assembly of Georgia:

A RESOLUTION

A Resolution to declare the Supreme Court decisions of May 17, 1954 and May 31, 1955, in the school segregation cases, and all similar decisions, by the Supreme Court null, void and of no effect; to declare that a contest of powers has arisen between the State of Georgia and the Supreme Court of the United States; to invoke the doctrine of interposition; and for other purposes.

BE IT RESOLVED BY THE HOUSE OF REPRESENTATIVES, THE SENATE CONCURRING, That the General Assembly of Georgia doth hereby unequivocally express a firm and determined resolution to maintain and defend the Constitution of the United States, and the Constitution of this State against every attempt, whether foreign or domestic, to undermine and destroy the fundamental principles, embodied in our basic law, by which the liberty of the people and the sovereignty of the States, in their proper spheres, have been long protected and assured;

* *Race Relations Law Reporter*, Vol. 1 (Nashville, 1956), pp. 438-40.

That the General Assembly of Georgia doth explicitly and pre-emptorily declare that it views the powers of the Federal Government as resulting solely from the compact, to which the States are parties, as limited by the plain sense and intention of the instrument creating that compact;

That the General Assembly of Georgia asserts that the powers of the Federal Government are valid only to the extent that these powers have been enumerated in the compact to which the various States assented originally and to which the States have assented in subsequent amendments validly adopted and ratified;

That the very nature of this basic compact, apparent upon its face, is that the ratifying States, parties thereto, have agreed voluntarily to surrender certain of their sovereign rights, but only certain of these sovereign rights, to a Federal Government thus constituted; and that all powers not delegated to the United States by the Constitution, nor prohibited by it to the States, have been reserved to the States respectively, or to the people;

That the State of Georgia has at no time surrendered to the General Government its rights to maintain racially separate public schools and other public facilities;

That the State of Georgia, in ratifying the Fourteenth Amendment to the Constitution, did not agree, nor did the other States ratifying the Fourteenth Amendment agree, that the power to operate racially separate public schools and other facilities was to be prohibited to them thereby;

And as evidence of such understanding, the General Assembly of Georgia notes that the very Congress that submitted the Fourteenth Amendment for ratification established separate schools in the District of Columbia and that in more than one instance the same State Legislatures that ratified the Fourteenth Amendment also provided for systems of racially separate public schools;

That the General Assembly of Georgia denies that the Supreme Court of the United States had the right which it asserted in the school cases decided by it on May 17, 1954, to enlarge the language and meaning of the compact by the States in an effort to withdraw from the States powers reserved to them and as duly exercised by them for almost a century;

That a question of contested power has arisen; the Supreme Court of the United States asserts, for its part, that the States did in fact prohibit unto themselves the power to maintain racially separate public institutions and the State of Georgia, for its part, asserts that it and its sister States have never surrendered such right;

That this assertion upon the part of the Supreme Court of the United States, accompanied by threats of coercion and compulsion against the sovereign States of this Union, constitutes a deliberate, palpable, and dangerous attempt by the Court to prohibit to the States certain rights and powers never surrendered by them;

That the General Assembly of Georgia asserts that whenever the General Government attempts to engage in the deliberate, palpable and dangerous exercise of powers not granted to it the States who are parties to the compact have the right, and are in duty bound, to interpose for arresting the progress of the evil, and for maintaining, within their respective limits the authorities, rights and liberties appertaining to them;

That failure on the part of this State thus to assert its clear rights would be construed as acquiescence in the surrender thereof; and that such submissive acquiescence to the seizure of one right would in the end lead to the surrender of all rights, and inevitably to the consolidation of the States into one sovereignty, contrary to the sacred compact by which this Union of States was created;

That the question of contested power asserted in this resolution is not within the province of the Court to determine because the Court itself seeks to usurp the powers which have been reserved to the States, and, therefore, under these circumstances, the judgment of all of the parties to the compact must be sought to resolve the question. The Supreme Court is not a party to the compact, but a creature of the compact and the question of contested power should not be settled by the creature seeking to usurp the power, but by the parties to the compact who are the people of the respective States in whom ultimate sovereignty finally reposes. . . .

That the Court was without jurisdiction of said cases because (1) the jurisdiction of the Court granted by the Constitution is limited to judicial cases in law and equity, and said cases were not of a judicial nature and character, nor did they involve controversies in law or equity, but, on the contrary, the great subjects of the controversy are of a legislative character, and not a judicial character, and are determinable only by the people themselves speaking through their legislative bodies; (2) the essential nature and effect of the proceedings relating exclusively to public schools operated by and under the authority of States, and pursuant to State laws and regulations, said cases were suits against the States, and the Supreme Court was without power or authority to try said cases, brought by individuals against States, because the Constitution forbids the Court to entertain suits by individuals against a State unless the State has consented to be sued;

That if said Court had had jurisdiction and authority to try and determine said cases, it was powerless to interfere with the operation of the public schools of States, because the Constitution of the United States does not confer upon the General Government any power or authority over such schools or over the subject of education, jurisdiction over these matters being reserved to the States, nor did the States by the Fourteenth Amendment authorize any interference on the part of the Judicial Department or any other department of the Federal Government with the operation by the States of such public schools as they might in their discretion see fit to establish and operate;

That by said cases the Court announces its power to adjudge State laws unconstitutional upon the basis of the Court's opinion of such laws as tested by rules of the inexact and speculative theories of psychological knowledge, which power and authority is beyond the jurisdiction of said Court;

That if the Court is permitted to exercise the power to judge the nature and effect of a law by supposed principles of psychological theory, and to hold the statute or Constitution of a State unconstitutional because of the opinions of the Judges as to its suitability, the States will have been destroyed, and the indestructible Union of Indestructible States established by the Constitution of the United States will have ceased to exist, and in its stead the Court will have created, without jurisdiction or authority from the people, one central government of total power;

That implementing its decision of May 17, 1954, said Court on May 31, 1955, upon further consideration of said cases, said:

"All provisions of Federal, State, or local law . . . must yield" to said decision of May 17, 1954; said Court thereby presuming arrogantly to give orders to the State of Georgia;

That it is clear that said Court has deliberately resolved to disobey the Constitution of the United States, and to flout and defy the Supreme Law of the Land;

That the State of Georgia has the right to operate and maintain a public school system utilizing such educational methods therein as in her judgment are conducive to the welfare of those to be educated and the people of the State generally, this being a governmental responsibility which the State has assumed lawfully, and her rights in this respect have not in any wise been delegated to the Central Government, but, on the contrary, she and the other States have reserved such matters to themselves by the terms of the Tenth Amendment. Being possessed of this lawful right, the State of Georgia is possessed of power to repel every unlawful interference therewith;

That the duty and responsibility of protecting life, property and the priceless possessions of freedom rests upon the Government of Georgia as to all those within her territorial limits. The State alone has this responsibility. Laboring under this high obligation she is possessed of the means to effectuate it. It is the duty of the State in flagrant cases such as this to interpose its powers between its people and the effort of said Court to assert an unlawful dominion over them;

THEREFORE, BE IT FURTHER RESOLVED BY THE HOUSE OF REPRESENTATIVES, THE SENATE CONCURRING:

First: That said decisions and orders of the Supreme Court of the United States relating to separation of the races in the public institutions of a State as announced and promulgated by said Court on May 17, 1954, and May 31, 1955 are null, void and of no force or effect;

Second: That hereby there is declared the firm intention of this State to take all appropriate measures honorably and constitutionally available to the State, to avoid this illegal encroachment upon the rights of her people;

Third: That we urge upon our sister States firm and deliberate efforts upon their part to check this and further encroachment on the part of the General Government, and on the part of said Court through judicial legislation, upon the reserved powers of all the States, that by united efforts the States may be preserved;

Fourth: That a copy of this Resolution be transmitted by His Excellency The Governor to the Governor and Legislature of each of the other States, to the President of the United States, to each of the Houses of Congress, to Georgia's Representatives and Senators in the Congress, and to the Supreme Court of the United States for its information.

READING NO. 18

Cooper v. Aaron, 1958*

The Court's answer to the Southern claim that the states are not bound by the decisions of the Supreme Court is given in this case. In it the Court was presented directly with the argument that the governor and legislature of Arkansas were not bound by the decision invalidating school segregation. This contention was rejected in incisive terms. The categorical rejection was emphasized by the unusual rendering of the opinion in the names of each of the nine Justices.

Opinion of the Court by THE CHIEF JUSTICE, MR. JUSTICE BLACK, MR. JUSTICE FRANKFURTER, MR. JUSTICE DOUGLAS, MR. JUSTICE BURTON, MR. JUSTICE CLARK, MR. JUSTICE HARLAN, MR. JUSTICE BRENNAN, and MR. JUSTICE WHITTAKER.

As this case reaches us it raises questions of the highest importance to the maintenance of our federal system of government. It necessarily involves a claim by the Governor and Legislature of a State that there is no duty on state officials to obey federal court orders resting on this Court's considered interpretation of the United States Constitution. Specifically it involves actions by the Governor and Legislature of Arkansas upon the premise that they are not bound by our holding in *Brown* v. *Board of Education*, 347 U. S. 483. That holding was that the Fourteenth Amendment forbids States to use their governmental powers to bar children on racial grounds from attending schools where there is state participation through any arrangement, management, funds or property. We are urged to uphold a suspension of the Little Rock School Board's plan to do away with segregated public schools in Little Rock until state laws and efforts to upset and nullify our holding in *Brown* v. *Board of Education* have been further challenged and tested in the courts. We reject these contentions. . . .

* 358 U.S. 1, 4-19 (1958).

The controlling legal principles are plain. The command of the Fourteenth Amendment is that no "State" shall deny to any person within its jurisdiction the equal protection of the laws. "A State acts by its legislative, its executive, or its judicial authorities. It can act in no other way. The constitutional provision, therefore, must mean that no agency of the State, or of the officers or agents by whom its powers are exerted, shall deny to any person within its jurisdiction the equal protection of the laws. Whoever, by virtue of public position under a State government, . . . denies or takes away the equal protection of the laws, violates the constitutional inhibition; and as he acts in the name and for the State, and is clothed with the State's power, his act is that of the State. This must be so, or the constitutional prohibition has no meaning." *Ex parte Virginia,* 100 U. S. 339, 347. Thus the prohibitions of the Fourteenth Amendment extend to all action of the State denying equal protection of the laws; whatever the agency of the State taking the action, see *Virginia* v. *Rives,* 100 U. S. 313; *Pennsylvania* v. *Board of Directors of City Trusts of Philadelphia,* 353 U. S. 230; *Shelley* v. *Kraemer,* 334 U. S. 1; or whatever the guise in which it is taken, see *Derrington* v. *Plummer,* 240 F. 2d 922; *Department of Conservation and Development* v. *Tate,* 231 F. 2d 615. In short, the constitutional rights of children not to be discriminated against in school admission on grounds of race or color declared by this Court in the *Brown* case can neither be nullified openly and directly by state legislators or state executive or judicial officers, nor nullified indirectly by them through evasive schemes for segregation whether attempted "ingeniously or ingenuously." *Smith* v. *Texas,* 311 U. S. 128, 132.

What has been said, in the light of the facts developed, is enough to dispose of the case. However, we should answer the premise of the actions of the Governor and Legislature that they are not bound by our holding in the *Brown* case. It is necessary only to recall some basic constitutional propositions which are settled doctrine.

Article VI of the Constitution makes the Constitution the "supreme Law of the Land." In 1803, Chief Justice Marshall, speaking for a unanimous Court, referring to the Constitution as "the fundamental and paramount law of the nation," declared in the notable case of *Marbury* v. *Madison,* 1 Cranch 137, 177, that "It is emphatically the province and duty of the judicial department to say what the law is." This decision declared the basic principle that the federal judiciary is supreme in the exposition of the law of the Constitution, and that principle has ever since been respected by this Court and the Country as a permanent and indispensable feature of our constitutional system. It follows that the interpretation of the Fourteenth Amendment enunciated by this Court in the *Brown* case is the supreme law of the land, and Art. VI of the Constitution makes it of binding effect on the States "any Thing in the Constitution or Laws of any State to the Contrary notwithstanding." Every state legislator and executive and judicial officer is solemnly committed by oath taken pursuant to Art. VI, cl. 3, "to support this Constitution." Chief Justice Taney, speaking for a unanimous Court in 1859, said that this requirement reflected the framers' "anxiety to preserve it [the Constitution] in full force, in all its powers, and to guard against resistance to or evasion of its authority, on the part of a State. . . ." *Ableman* v. *Booth,* 21 How. 506, 524.

No state legislator or executive or judicial officer can war against the Constitution without violating his undertaking to support it. Chief Justice Marshall spoke for a unanimous Court in saying that: "If the legislatures of the several states may, at will, annul the judgments of the courts of the United States, and destroy the rights acquired under those judgments, the constitution itself becomes a solemn mockery . . . ." *United States* v. *Peters,* 5 Cranch 115, 136. A Governor who asserts a power to nullify a federal court order is similarly restrained. If he had such power, said Chief Justice Hughes, in 1932, also for a unanimous Court, "it is manifest that the fiat of a state Governor, and not the Constitution of the United States, would be the supreme law of the land; that the restrictions of the Federal Constitution upon the exercise of state power would be but impotent phrases. . . ." *Sterling* v. *Constantin,* 287 U. S. 378, 397-398.

READING NO. 19

Reynolds v. Sims, 1964*

Few decisions of the Court have had as great practical impact as its recent decisions requiring equality in legislative apportionment. The key cases have been Baker v. Carr *(1962), sustaining judicial jurisdiction to decide a claim that a legislative apportionment violated the equal protection clause, and this case, spelling out what that clause demands in specific cases. The Warren opinion paints broadly, in a manner reminiscent of Marshall and Taney, a wholesale requirement of complete equality in the political process. The decision strikingly demonstrates the practical impact of the Court, for it has already worked a virtual revolution in the distribution of political power.*

Mr. Chief Justice Warren delivered the opinion of the Court.

Involved in these cases are an appeal and two cross-appeals from a decision of the Federal District Court for the Middle District of Alabama holding invalid, under the Equal Protection Clause of the Federal Constitution, the existing and two legislatively proposed plans for the apportionment of seats in the two houses of the Alabama Legislature, and ordering into effect a temporary reapportionment plan comprised of parts of the proposed but judicially disapproved measures. . . .

Undeniably the Constitution of the United States protects the right of all qualified citizens to vote, in state as well as in federal elections. A consistent line of decisions by this Court in cases involving attempts to deny or restrict the right of suffrage has made this indelibly clear. It has been repeatedly recognized that all qualified voters have a constitutionally protected right to vote, *Ex parte Yarbrough,* 110 U. S. 651, and to have their votes counted, *United States* v. *Mosley,* 238 U. S. 383. In *Mosley* the Court stated that it is "as equally unquestionable that the right to have one's vote counted is as open to

* 377 U.S. 533, 536-68 (1964).

protection . . . as the right to put a ballot in a box." 238 U. S., at 386. The right to vote can neither be denied outright, *Guinn* v. *United States,* 238 U. S. 347, *Lane* v. *Wilson,* 307 U. S. 268, nor destroyed by alteration of ballots, see *United States* v. *Classic,* 313 U. S. 299, 315, nor diluted by ballot-box stuffing, *Ex parte Siebold,* 100 U. S. 371, *United States* v. *Saylor,* 322 U. S. 385. As the Court stated in *Classic,* "Obviously included within the right to choose, secured by the Constitution, is the right of qualified voters within a state to cast their ballots and have them counted . . . ." 313 U. S., at 315. Racially based gerrymandering, *Gomillion* v. *Lightfoot,* 364 U. S. 339, and the conducting of white primaries, *Nixon* v. *Herndon,* 273 U. S. 536, *Nixon* v. *Condon,* 286 U. S. 73, *Smith* v. *Allwright,* 321 U. S. 649, *Terry* v. *Adams,* 345 U. S. 461, both of which result in denying to some citizens their right to vote, have been held to be constitutionally impermissible. And history has seen a continuing expansion of the scope of the right of suffrage in this country. The right to vote freely for the candidate of one's choice is of the essence of a democratic society, and any restrictions on that right strike at the heart of representative government. And the right of suffrage can de denied by a debasement or dilution of the weight of a citizen's vote just as effectively as by wholly prohibiting the free exercise of the franchise. . . .

Legislators represent people, not trees or acres. Legislators are elected by voters, not farms or cities or economic interests. As long as ours is a representative form of government, and our legislatures are those instruments of government elected directly by and directly representative of the people, the right to elect legislators in a free and unimpaired fashion is a bedrock of our political system. It could hardly be gainsaid that a constitutional claim had been asserted by an allegation that certain otherwise qualified voters had been entirely prohibited from voting for members of their state legislature. And, if a State should provide that the votes of citizens in one part of the State should be given two times, or five times, or 10 times the weight of votes of citizens in another part of the State, it could hardly be contended that the right to vote of those residing in the disfavored areas had not effectively diluted. It would appear extraordinary to suggest that a State could be constitutionally permitted to enact a law providing that certain of the State's voters could vote two, five, or 10 times for their legislative representatives, while voters living elsewhere could vote only once. And it is inconceivable that a state law to the effect that, in counting votes for legislators, the votes of citizens in one part of the State would be multiplied by two, five, or 10, while the votes of persons in another area would be counted only at face value, could be constitutionally sustainable. Of course, the effect of state legislative districting schemes which give the same number of representatives to unequal numbers of constituents is identical. Overweighting and overvaluation of the votes of those living here has the certain effect of dilution and undervaluation of the votes of those living there. The resulting discrimination against those individual voters living in disfavored areas is easily demonstrable mathematically. Their right to vote is simply not the same right to vote as that of those living in a favored part of the State. Two, five, or 10 of them must vote before the effect of their voting is equivalent to that of their favored neighbor. Weighting the votes of citizens differently, by any method or means, merely because of where they happen to reside, hardly seems justifiable. One must be ever aware that the Constitution forbids "sophisticated as well as simple-minded modes of discrimination." . . .

State legislatures are, historically, the fountainhead of representative government in this country. A number of them have their roots in colonial times, and substantially antedate the creation of our Nation and our Federal Government. In fact, the first formal stirrings of American political independence are to be found, in large part, in the views and actions of several of the colonial legislative bodies. With the birth of our National Government, and the adoption and ratification of the Federal Constitution, state legislatures retained a most important place in our Nation's governmental structure. But representative government is in essence self-government through the medium of elected representatives of the people, and each and every citizen has an inalienable right to full and effective participation in the political processes of his State's legislative bodies. Most citizens can achieve this participation only as qualified voters through the election of legislators to represent them. Full and effective participation by all citizens in state government requires, therefore, that each citizen have an equally effective voice in the election of members of his state legislature. Modern and viable state government needs, and the Constitution demands, no less.

Logically, in a society ostensibly grounded on representative government, it would seem reasonable that a majority of the people of a State could elect a majority of that State's legislators. To conclude differently, and to sanction minority control of state legislative bodies, would appear to deny majority rights in a way that far surpasses any possible denial of minority rights that might otherwise be thought to result. Since legislatures are responsible for enacting laws by which all citizens are to be governed, they should be bodies which are collectively responsive to the popular will. And the concept of equal protection has been traditionally viewed as requiring the uniform treatment of persons standing in the same relation to the governmental action questioned or challenged. With respect to the allocation of legislative representation, all voters, as citizens of a State, stand in the same relation regardless of where they live. Any suggested criteria for the differentiation of citizens are insufficient to justify any discrimination, as to the weight of their votes, unless relevant to the permissible purposes of legislative apportionment. Since the achieving of fair and effective representation for all citizens is concededly the basic aim of legislative apportionment, we conclude that the Equal Protection Clause guarantees the opportunity for equal participation by all voters in the election of state legislators. Diluting the weight of votes because of place of residence impairs basic constitutional rights under the Fourteenth Amendment. . . . To the extent that a citizen's right to vote is debased, he is that much less a citizen. The fact that an individual lives here or there is not a legitimate reason for overweighting or diluting the efficacy of his vote. The complexions of societies and civilizations change, often with amazing rapidity. A nation once primarily rural in character becomes predominantly urban. Representation schemes once fair and equitable become archaic and outdated. But the basic principle of representative government remains, and must remain, unchanged —the weight of a citizen's vote cannot be made to depend on where he lives. Population is, of necessity, the starting point for consideration and the controlling criterion for judgment in legislative apportionment controversies. A citizen, a qualified voter, is no more nor no less so because he lives in the city or on the farm. This is the clear and strong command of our Constitution's Equal Protection Clause. This is an essential part of the concept of a government of laws and not men. This is at the heart of Lincoln's vision of "government of the people, by the people, [and] for the people." The Equal Protection Clause demands no less than substantially equal state legislative representation for all citizens, of all places as well as of all races. . . .

We hold that, as a basic constitutional standard, the Equal Protection Clause requires that the seats in both houses of a bicameral state legislature must be apportioned on a population basis. Simply stated, an individual's right to vote for state legislators is unconstitutionally impaired when its weight is in a substantial fashion diluted when compared with votes of citizens living in other parts of the State. Since, under neither the existing apportionment provisions nor either of the proposed plans was either of the houses of the Alabama Legislature apportioned on a population basis, the District Court correctly held that all three of these schemes were constitutionally invalid.

READING NO. 20

Justice Clark on the Court in Operation*

In this address, a member of the Court presents us with a rare insider's picture of the Court in operation. In particular, he explains the procedure followed in dealing with cases after the public proceedings, culminating in argument in the courtroom, are closed. The decision-making process in conference is the key to the Court's work, and even close students of the Court are unaware of exactly what happens during it. In this reading we are given a privileged look into the inner sanctum of our constitutional law.

What occurs between the day of argument and the time of decision? I often wondered myself as I sat at the Bar of the Court in the chair reserved for the Attorney General. After sitting there for over four years it became my good fortune to become one of the eighty-nine lawyers in American history to learn at first hand what goes on behind the heavy purple curtain that separates the open courtroom from the closed conference chamber. . . .

In this connection I am reminded that my choice of subjects—the unsung works of the Court—was influenced by what in motion picture parlance might be called a "theme song" of Chief Justice Hughes. Before each of the annual meetings of the American Law Institute during his incumbency he spoke of the administrative problems facing the Court, most of which he feared the lawyers "but little understood." He pointed out that some lawyers thought there was some "mystery about [the certiorari] work" of the Court, which mystery the Chief belied and insisted "should be dispelled." He found that "some think that applications . . . are distributed among the Justices ratably. . . . [O]thers think the Justice assigned to a Circuit deals with applications from the Circuit." My associate, the beloved Robert H.

* T. Clark, *The Supreme Court Conference,* 19 *Federal Rules Decisions* (1956), 303-10.

Jackson, some twenty years later added with a twinkle in his eye: "[A] suspicion has grown at the bar that the law clerks [of which each of us have two, save the Chief, who has three] constitute a kind of junior court which decides the fate of certiorari petitions. This idea of the law clerk's influence," said Mr. Justice Jackson, "gave rise to a lawyer's waggish statement that the Senate no longer need bother about confirmation of Justices but ought to confirm the appointment of law clerks." In fact, during my seven years on the Court I have been asked by prominent lawyers, who should know better, to please speak to my law clerks about their petitions.

All of you know what happens in our courtroom. Many of you are familiar with the details of our schedule calling for argument of counsel during a two week period, followed by two weeks of recess. Argument sessions run from Monday through Thursday. Each party at argument is allowed one hour, unless by reason of the nature of the question the time is cut in half. On Friday we sit in conference. The period of recess is devoted to opinion writing and the study of appeals and certiorari petitions.

How much time does each Justice have at conference on Friday of each argument week? Does conference discussion shed more heat than light? What is the demeanor of the Justices? Let us go from the austere courtroom—from the friezes depicting the lawgivers, the Greek Ionic columns and the heavy draperies—to the oak-paneled conference chamber and see what is going on there. Over the mantle facing the large rectangular conference table is a portrait of Chief Justice Marshall, the fourth Chief Justice by number, but the first in stature. Around this table are nine chairs, each bearing the nameplate of a member of the Court. At the east end sits the Chief Justice, and at the west, Mr. Justice Black, the senior Associate Justice. On the sides, in order of seniority, sit the remaining Associate Justices. Bookcases from floor to ceiling line the walls containing all the opinions of the Federal courts. Here the Court meets in conference at eleven A. M. on each Friday during or preceding an argument week, and rarely does it rise before 5:30 P.M.

Only the Justices are present at conference. There are no clerks, no stenographers, no secretaries, no pages. This long-established practice is based on reason. The Court must carry on these Friday conferences in absolute secrecy, otherwise its judgments might become prematurely known and the whole process of decision destroyed. We therefore guard its secrets closely. There must be no leak. Scores of years ago the Court was convinced that there was a leak. At that time two page boys waited on the Justices within the conference room. After considerable investigation it was decided that the only possible leak was through one of these lads. After all, no one else was present save the Justices! So, since that day, no page—no person other than the Justices themselves—has ever attended a conference. And this despite the fact that thereafter a member of the bar advised the Court that it was he who had provided the "leak." Basing his conclusion of the outcome of a case purely on an educated guess, he had sold a block of stock in a corporation involved in the litigation on the very morning of the decision. His broker told another of the sale leading to a run on the stock. But leak or no leak, the Court ever since has stuck to the practice that only Justices are present. It was said by Woodrow Wilson that "our democratic state was not a piece of developed theory but a piece of developed habit. It was not created by mere aspirations or by new faith—it was built up by slow custom." This and other traditions of the Court lead me to the observation that the President's adage applies equally to the Court.

Upon entering the conference room, each Justice shakes hands with those present, another custom dating generations back. We first take out our assignment sheets or lists for the day. As you know, the only power of the Court is to decide lawsuits between litigants with real interests at stake. The Court can proceed only through the judicial process. This precludes the making of advisory opinions, even to the President. The Court is therefore a passive instrument. Still the Court decided over 1800 questions last term. There was an average of 71 cases on each list covering the twenty-six conferences held during the term; the longest list included 331 cases, the shortest 38. Our conferences last an average of 6 hours, so this would allow on the average about five minutes to each item on the list or half a minute to each Justice. Perhaps this limited time brought Mr. Justice McReynolds to the conclusion that an "overspeaking judge is no well-tuned cymbal." However, the Court is saved from being hopelessly bogged down by the elimination by consent of those cases that no Justice finds worthy of discussion.

What type of cases come up for discussion? First, appeals, then petitions for certiorari, next in *forma pauperis* cases, and, more important than all, the cases argued previously in the courtroom. The Court always decides the latter cases the same week in which they were argued. I have made a hurried study of the legal problems presented last term. Aside from 13 original cases involving controversies between a third of our States, as well as the United States, we passed on 1831 cases. They posed legal questions running from adoption to zoning. As De Tocqueville predicted back in 1832, some of these were political questions turned, though sometimes clumsily, into judicial issues. There were questions concerning the Constitution, statutory construction, individual and States rights, Indians, labor, taxes, executive powers, contempt, seamen, railroad workers, subversives, bar applicants, as well as a host of other subjects.

The Chief Justice starts the conference by calling the first case on the list and then discussing it. He then yields to the senior Associate Justice and on down the line seniority-wise until each Justice who wishes to be heard has spoken. There is no time limitation. The order is never interrupted nor is the speaker. Another tale going the rounds of the Court has to do with a conference of many terms back while the late Justices Harlan and Holmes were on the Court. Harlan was presenting his view of a case with which Holmes evidently did not agree. In the midst of Harlan's argument, Holmes interrupted with the sharp remark, "That won't wash! That won't wash!" Justice Holmes often greeted Justice Harlan as "my strong hearted friend," but he had never chided him about his legal conclusions. Harlan too, was strong minded and never turned away from a fight. In this regard his opinions show that he wielded a wicked pair of horns and often got his adversary out on both of them. Holmes, on the other hand, was the rapier type that cut so quickly one did not know his head was off until he attempted to turn it. Fortunately, the Chief Justice at the time was Melville Fuller. He had already discussed the case and his position was similar to that of Harlan. When the diminutive but courageous, silver-haired, handlebar-mustached Chief Justice realized that all was not well between his brothers he quickly answered Holmes' "That won't wash," with a cheery "Well, I'm scrubbing away, anyhow." A tense situation passed over during the ensuing laughter.

After discussion of a case a vote is taken. We each have available a large docket book, evidently, from its appearance, handed down to us by the first of the Justices. It has a hinge on its flyleaf which is kept locked. There we keep a record of the votes. Ever since John Marshall's day the formal vote begins with the junior Justice and moves up through the ranks of seniority, the Chief Justice voting last. Hence the juniors are not influenced by the vote of their elders! While it takes five votes to decide a case, it takes only four to grant a writ of certiorari. In this manner, as Justice Van Devanter explained to the Congress back in 1925, the Court makes certain that any case deserving argument is afforded it. I might point out here that only sixteen percent of the petitions filed last term were granted. Less than two percent were state court cases. As the late revered Chief Justice Vinson said, "The Supreme Court has never been primarily concerned with the correction of errors in lower court decisions." The certiorari function, he continued, "is not simply to do justice between the parties. Everyone who comes here has had one trial and one appeal already." The purpose of the establishment of one Supreme National Tribunal was in the words of Chief Justice John Rutledge, "to secure the national rights and the uniformity of judgments." That is our mission. When you do not get four votes and certiorari is denied, it means your case did not come within the rule—not that the result is right.

As you see from this routine, each Justice who does not disqualify himself passes on every piece of business coming to the Court. In some matters Justices excuse themselves. This is always noted. Perhaps they were connected with the litigation before it reached the Court, had some interests in its result, or did not hear the argument because of unavoidable absence.

I wish to emphasize here that the Court does not function by means of committees or panels. Some lawyers think a small committee of Justices passes on their petitions for certiorari. This is not true. Each Justice passes on each petition, each item, no matter how drawn, in longhand, by typewriter, or on a press. Our Constitution, as Brother Jackson has pointed out, "vests the judicial power in only 'one Supreme Court.'" This does not permit Supreme Court action by committees, panels, or sections. The method that the Justices use in meeting an enormous caseload such as last term varies. There is one uniform rule: Judging is not delegated. Each Justice studies each case in sufficient detail to resolve the question without leaving any doubt in his mind.

After the vote is recorded in argued cases there remains the task of writing the opinion for the Court. At the conclusion of the conference the cases are assigned for writing. The Chief Justice assigns those in which he has voted with the majority and the senior Justice voting with the majority the remainder. This has always been the rule. People often ask about the powers and duties of the Chief Justice. While it is not the purpose of this paper to cover that subject I might say that as to conference matters, aside from the duty of assigning opinions, the Chief Justice has no more authority than other members of the Court. The Chief Justice, of course, presides and initiates discussion, as a general rule, but has only one vote. However, the assignment of opinions is a most important duty. The manner of assignment varies as to courts. In New York State it goes by rotation. In one State, I am told, it goes by chance, while in others by subject matter.

When one starts to write an opinion for the Supreme Court of the United States he learns the full meaning of the statement of Rufus Choate that "one cannot drop the Greek alphabet to the ground and pick up the Iliad." It takes the most painstaking research and care. Mr. Justice Cardozo was not far wrong when he said, "A Judge must be a historian and prophet all in one." In the average case an opinion requires three weeks work in preparation. When the author concludes that he has an unanswerable document, it is printed in the print shop in the Supreme Court building and circulated to each of the Justices. Then the fur begins to fly. Returns come in, some favorable and many otherwise. In controversial cases, and all have some touches of controversy, the process often takes months. The cases are often discussed by the majority both before and after circulation. The final form of the opinion is agreed upon at the Friday conferences. Of course, any Justice may dissent or write his own views on a case. These are likewise circulated long before the opinion of the majority is announced.

The practice of a majority opinion with dissents and concurrences, does not conform with the European practice. Theirs resembles our *per curiams*. Our system may be the preferable one, but it presents practical difficulties. Mr. Justice Cardozo expressed the view that "comparatively speaking the dissenter is irresponsible. The spokesman of the Court is cautious, timid, fearful of the vivid word, the heightened phrase. . . . Not so the dissenter. . . . For the moment he is the gladiator making a last stand against the lions." For the most part the strong dissent forces the majority to take a more extreme position. Witness Chief Justice Taney in the *Dred Scott* case where the extreme statements found in the published opinion were inserted by the Chief Justice only after Mr. Justice McLean had circulated his dissent. As Brother Jackson says, "the true test of a judge is his influence in leading, not in opposing his Court." Laymen are constantly troubled by the divisions of opinion on the Court. Even lawyers decry it, particularly when they come out on what they believe to be the short end. Differences of opinion must be expected on legal questions as on other subjects. Every newspaper that is published reflects differences not only in reporting but in editorials. Clergymen differ on theology. Professors argue over philosophy. Physicists tangle on physical phenomena and doctors are at variance not only on diagnosis but on cure. The history of progress is filled with many pages of disagreement. Why, therefore, in the words of President E. Smythe Gambrell expect "the most influential men . . . on the bench . . . trained in a different philosophy and matured in a different climate" to have the same thoughts and views? They don't and they won't! As President Gambrell so aptly said, "The challenge of serving as umpire in the Federal system calls forth all the powers of the intellect, of the understanding, and of vision. It demands a sense of history and a discerning recognition of the relative competencies and capacities of the two levels of government."

To perform the task outlined by President Gambrell the mind must not be parboiled in formula for in the words of Mr. Justice Holmes, that "is a slumber that, prolonged, means death." No, to perform this task the founders created a human institution—

courts—and placed them in charge of human beings who like all such creatures are "on the dubious waves of error tost." In this respect judges are unlike that "certain French lady", mentioned by Benjamin Franklin in his address to the Constitutional Convention, who, while in a dispute with her sister expostulated: "I don't know how it happens, sister, but I meet with nobody—but myself—that's always in the right." But despite the differences and the conflicts there is one thing on which all agree and that is every man's right to disagree. Only by practicing this in full measure can truth ultimately be found. There will be, as always, some heat. Among judges, however, there is no contest, not even a "petty quarrel," but only a sincere and continuing effort to arrive at truth—at justice. As my Brother Frankfurter has so well put it: "What is essential [in judging] is . . . first and foremost, humility and an understanding of the range of the problems and [one's] own inadequacy in dealing with them: disinterestedness, allegiance to nothing except the search, amid tangled words, amid limited insights; loyalty and allegiance to nothing except the effort to find [that] path through precedent, through policy, through history, through [one's] own gifts of insight to the best judgment that a poor fallible creature can arrive at in that most difficult of all tasks, the adjudication between man and man, between man and state, through reason called law."

READING NO. 21

The Court's Work, October 1965*

While the work of the Court can scarcely be understood in statistical terms alone, a student should have some idea of the number of cases dealt with by the high tribunal. The statistics given cover the term starting in October 1965 and ending in June 1966. Disposition of the vast number of cases is possible only because the Court has discretionary control over its docket. Since 1925 appeals as of right have been sharply limited and almost all cases reach the Court through certiorari, which the justices have discretionary power to grant to deny. The vast majority of cases are disposed of by the simple denial of certiorari. The Court is essentially a tribunal to settle only such questions as it deems to involve a sufficient public concern to warrant decision by the highest bench in the land.

The business of the Term involved a total of 3284 cases on the dockets as compared with 2662 in the 1964 Term and 2779 in the 1963 Term (these and related statistics are taken from the Clerk's final statistics—see accompanying table *Final Statistics for Last Three Terms*). Cases argued totaled 131 (as compared with 122 in the 1964 Term and 144 in the 1963 Term), of which 122 were disposed of by 97 Opinions of the Court (105 were disposed of by 91 Opinions in the prior term) and 8 by Per Curiam Opinions (as compared with 17 in the prior term), with 1 restored for reargument. Of the 97 Opinions of the Court and 8 Per Curiams, 43 or about 41% were unanimous or involved concurrences only (as compared with 30% last Term and 41% in each of the preceding terms), and 62 or about 59% involved dissents from holding or major doctrine (as compared with 70% last Term and 59% each of the two preceding terms) thereby returning to the higher percentage of unanimous results that prevailed in the two terms before last. The decisions involving

* G. K. Reiblich, *Summary of October 1965 Term, 86 Supreme Court Reporter* (St. Paul, 1967), pp. 245-48.

dissents were distributed about as follows (with variances possible according to the treatment given to partial dissents, and some dissents from summary Per Curiams which are not fully reflected here although counted in the total of dissenting votes for the term): thirteen 5-4, one 4-3, ten 6-3, two 5-2, three 6-2, thirteen 7-2, eight 7-1, and twelve 8-1. The total dissenting votes were 162 as compared with 152 last term but they relate to a larger number of majority opinions and often are expressed in opinions which concur in the disposition of the case in which they appear. To this reviewer, their pattern suggests a strengthen- rather than any weakening of the control of the Court by the liberal majority led by Chief Justice Warren as earlier referred to and discussed.

The dissenting opinions and votes as compared with last term were as follows: Mr. Justice Harlan 38 dissenting votes and 15 dissenting opinions (30 and 12 last term); Mr. Justice Black 26 dissenting votes and 9 dissenting opinions (30 and 12 last term); Mr. Justice Douglas 25 dissenting votes and 10 dissenting opinions (27 and 10 last term); Mr. Justice Stewart 23 dissenting votes and 7 dissenting opinions (22 and 8 last term); Mr. Justice White 15 dissenting votes and 6 dissenting opinions (10 and 5 last term); Mr. Justice Fortas 15 dissenting votes and 6 dissenting opinions (as related to 15 and 9 for Mr. Justice Goldberg last term); Mr. Justice Clark 9 dissenting votes and 3 dissenting opinions (11 and 2 last term); Mr. Chief Justice Warren 6 dissenting votes and 1 dissenting opinion (5 and 0 last term); Mr. Justice Brennan 5 dissenting votes and 0 dissenting opinions (2 and 0 last term).

The 97 Opinions of the Court were not as evenly distributed as last term, with 13 by Mr. Justice Brennan, 12 by each of Justices Douglas and Stewart, 11 by each of Justices Black, Clark and White, 10 by Mr. Justice Fortas, 9 by Mr. Chief Justice Warren, and 8 by Mr. Justice Harlan. There were 32 concurring opinions as compared with 45 last term, 15 separate opinions as compared with 14 last year, and 57 dissenting opinions as compared with 58 last term. The total number of opinions delivered was 201 as compared with 208 last term, and only 8 Per Curiams disposing of matters argued as compared with 17 last term.

The total number of cases disposed of was 2693 as compared with 2180 last term. The Court adjourned on June 20, 1966, two weeks later than last term's date of June 7. The cases remaining on the dockets were considerably above last term, continuing the upward trend from last term. It is to be expected that an activist Court will generate business for itself, at least during a period of changing constitutional doctrine.

FINAL STATISTICS FOR LAST THREE TERMS

(Comparing Clerk's Statistics 6/23/64, 6/8/65, 6/23/66)

Appellate Docket	1963	1964	1965
Cases on docket to date	1238	1247	1436
Cases disposed of during term	1036	1027	1182
Certiorari denied or dismissed	733	791	900
Off merits	303	236	282
Certiorari granted	118	116	124
Set for argument	74	85	88
Summarily affirmed, reversed or vacated	44	31	36*
Appeals dismissed	76	53*	69
Appeals noted or postponed and set for argument	31	34	40
Appeals—summarily affirmed, reversed or vacated	41	33	49

Miscellaneous Docket			
Cases on docket to date	1532	1404	1831
Cases disposed of during term	1374	1151	1502
Certiorari denied or dismissed	1093	927	1271
Certiorari granted:	69	21	43
Set for argument	11	7	25
Summarily affirmed, reversed or vacated	58	14	18
Appeals dismissed	30	22	37
Appeals noted, and set for argument	0	0	3
Appeals—summarily affirmed, reversed or vacated	1	2	0
Other applications denied or withdrawn, etc.	180	178	147
Other applications granted	1	1	1

Cases argued and submitted during term	144	122**	131**
Disposed of by written opinions	123	105**	122**
Disposed of by per curiam opinions	20	17**	8
Restored for reargument	1	0	1
Number of written opinions	111	91**	97**
Cases available for argument and time allotted:	65	65	91
Next term: 91 cases (104 Hrs) (26 Da) (6½ Wks)			
Past term: 65 cases (74 Hrs) (18½ Da) (4⅝ Wks)			
Admissions to the Bar	3184	2735	3331

Distribution of Cases Remaining on Dockets

Original cases	7	9	8
Appellate cases on merits	81	86	91
Petitions for certiorari	121	134	163
Miscellaneous docket applications	158	253	329

* Includes one case remanded.
** Includes 2 original cases in the current term and 3 original cases in the last term, the opinion of one of which was per curiam last term.

NOTE: Last term the Court adjourned on June 7, 1965.
This term the Court adjourned on June 20, 1966.

OPINIONS AND DISSENTING VOTES

October Terms, 1964 and 1965

Number of Printed Opinions and Memoranda Filed During October Terms, 1964 and 1965

	Opinions of the Court		Concurring Opinions		Dissenting Opinions		Dissenting Votes		Separate Opinions		Totals	
	OT '65	OT '65	OT '64	OT '65	OT '64	OT '65	OT '64	OT '65	OT '64	OT '65	OT '64	OT '65
WARREN, C. J.	10	9	1	0	0	1	5	6	0	1	11	11
BLACK, J.	10	11	4	0	12	9	30	26	2	3	28	23
DOUGLAS, J.	10	12	7	6	10	10	27	25	2	0	29	28
CLARK, J.	12	11*	2	2	2	3	11	9	1	0	17	16
HARLAN, J.	10	8	12	10	12	15	30	38	3	9	37	42
BRENNAN, J.	10	13*	2	4	0	0	2	5	1	1	13	18
STEWART, J.	9	12	6	3	8	7	22	23	1	0	24	22
WHITE, J.	10*	11	4	4	5	6	10	15	1	1	20	22
GOLDBERG, J.	10	0	7	0	9	0	15	0	3	0	29	0
FORTAS, J.	0	10*	0	3	0	6	0	15	0	0	0	19
	91	97	45	32	58	57	152	162	14	15	208	201

* Includes opinions announcing the judgments of the Court.

OPINIONS PER CURIAM in argued cases—O.T. 1964—17; O.T. 1965—8; including one motion in 1964 Term for leave to file complaint granted in original action.

NOTE: Memorandum opinions of individual justices in chamber matters, dissenting to *per curiams* in cases not argued, on the denial of petitions for certiorari, etc., are not included in the above figures. Of the 131 cases argued during October Term, 1965, 122 were decided by signed opinions and 8 by *per curiams*. One case was set for reargument. This table is taken from the Clerk's statistics of June 24, 1966, except for the dissenting votes which are taken by count from all opinions and *per curiams* reported in the text of 86 S.Ct. Reporter, including votes in partial dissent, but excluding memorandum decisions.

READING NO. 22

A Justice Leaves the Court, 1962 and 1965*

The Court is a collegiate body whose members call each other "brethren." In so small and closely knit a group the departure of a justice is always an event of consequence, particularly where he has become as established a part of the institution as did Felix Frankfurter. The letters that follow were occasioned by Justice Frankfurter's retirement and the address of the Chief Justice by his death. The reader should observe both the place of an individual justice, like Frankfurter, and his position as a link in a chain of justices that stretches back to the very founding of the Republic. It is the Court's institutional tradition that enables it "to get on with our always unfinished work."

SUPREME COURT OF THE UNITED STATES.
MONDAY, OCTOBER 1, 1962.

Present: MR. CHIEF JUSTICE WARREN, MR. JUSTICE BLACK, MR. JUSTICE DOUGLAS, MR. JUSTICE CLARK, MR. JUSTICE HARLAN, MR. JUSTICE BRENNAN, MR. JUSTICE STEWART and MR. JUSTICE WHITE.

THE CHIEF JUSTICE said:

With the concurrence of my colleagues, I announce with regret the retirement of Mr. Justice Frankfurter who has served this Court with distinction for the past 24 years.

All of us, with the exception of Mr. Justice White, have had the pleasure of serving for years with him, and we exceedingly regret that the condition of his health compelled his retirement. We are reconciled to the situation, however, by the opinion of

* 371 U.S. vii-xiii (1963); 380 U.S. vii-viii (1965).

his doctor that if he is relieved of his arduous Court work he will still have years of usefulness to the profession to which he has been devoted for 60 years. We look forward to such a speedy and complete recovery because he has so much to give from his vast experience.

As scholar, teacher, public servant, enlightened critic, and member of this Court for almost a quarter of a century, he has already made a contribution to our jurisprudence rarely equalled in the life of our Court. Through each of these facets of his long and notable career, he looms large in the history of our country and we, his colleagues, have been the most favored beneficiaries of his wisdom and his fellowship. These we may continue to enjoy because our association with him is not ended. It will continue unabated in another form.

Our appreciation of that association and for his great service to the Court is amplified in a letter to him which, with his response and the exchange of letters between him and the President on the occasion of his retirement, will be spread upon the Minutes of the Court.

Supreme Court of the United States,
Chambers of The Chief Justice,
Washington 25, D. C., September 27, 1962.

Honorable Felix Frankfurter,
*Associate Justice of the Supreme Court, Retired,
Washington, D. C.*

Dear Justice Frankfurter:

As the opening day of our 1962 Term approaches, it becomes increasingly difficult for all of us to realize that you will not be in your accustomed chair, which you filled with such distinction and in such good fellowship with your colleagues for almost a quarter of a century.

All of us, except Mr. Justice White, our newest member, have served with you for years and we, more than any others, will feel the loss that comes from your retirement. We regret the necessity for it, but we reluctantly accept your decision because your doctor has told you and us that if this course is pursued there will be opened to you new avenues of usefulness to the profession to which you dedicated yourself 60 years ago.

Every one of those years was an eventful year for you as you strained every fiber of your mind and body to the administration of justice and to the welfare of the Court. Few men in the life of the Supreme Court have made contributions to its jurisprudence equal to your own. As a scholar, teacher, critic, public servant, and a member of the Court for 24 Terms, you have woven your philosophy of law and your conception of our institutions into its annals where all may read them and profit thereby.

Your retirement does not end our association. It merely changes the form of it. You will always be one of us, and after rest and relaxation from the rigors of the Court work restore you to health, we look forward to years of continued happy association with you. In the meantime, our best wishes for a rapid recovery will always be with you.

Sincerely,
EARL WARREN
HUGO L. BLACK
WM. O. DOUGLAS
TOM C. CLARK
JOHN M. HARLAN
WM. J. BRENNAN, JR.
POTTER STEWART
BYRON R. WHITE

SUPREME COURT OF THE UNITED STATES,
CHAMBERS OF JUSTICE FELIX FRANKFURTER,
Washington, D. C., September 28, 1962.

MY DEAR BRETHREN:

It would be unnatural for me not to address you thus, although you have been apprised that I have advised the President of my decision to retire as of August 28th, under the appropriate provisions of law, as an active member of the Court. I still address you as I do, for the endeavors which the business of the Court entails in the daily intimacy of our association have forged bonds of fellowship which cannot be abruptly severed.

A JUSTICE LEAVES THE COURT

The final manifestation of your fraternal feelings toward me, your letter of September 27th, your generous words of farewell, are a cheering close to our uniformly happy curial relations over the years, and I shall enduringly cherish your moving letter. Retiring from active membership on the Court of itself would involve a wrench in my life, but the fact is that I have served the Court in one professional way or another almost from the day that I ceased to be a law student, not merely during the years that I have actually been on the Bench.

My years on the Court have only deepened my conviction that its existence and functioning according to its best historic traditions are indispensable for the well-being of the nation. The nature of the issues which are involved in the legal controversies that are inevitable under our constitutional system does not warrant the nation to expect identity of views among the members of the Court regarding such issues, nor even agreement on the routes of thought by which decisions are reached. The nation is merely warranted in expecting harmony of aims among those who have been called to the Court. This means pertinacious pursuit of the processes of Reason in the disposition of the controversies that come before the Court. This presupposes intellectual disinterestedness in the analysis of the factors involved in the issues that call for decision. This in turn requires rigorous self-scrutiny to discover, with a view to curbing, every influence that may deflect from such disinterestedness.

I have spent happy years in my fellowship with you and I carry away the abiding memory of years of comradeship in grappling with problems worthy of the best in fallible men.

My best wishes for happy, long years for each of you and continued satisfying labors, and every good wish that the Court may continue its indispensable role in the evolution of our beloved nation.

With the happiest memories, I am

Sincerely and faithfully yours,
FELIX FRANKFURTER.

THE CHIEF JUSTICE AND ASSOCIATE JUSTICES OF
  THE SUPREME COURT OF THE UNITED STATES
  OF AMERICA.

SUPREME COURT OF THE UNITED STATES,
CHAMBERS OF JUSTICE FELIX FRANKFURTER,
Washington 25, D. C., August 28, 1962.

MY DEAR MR. PRESIDENT:

Pursuant to the provisions of 28 U. S. C. Section 371(b), 68 Stat. 12, I hereby retire at the close of this day from regular active service as an Associate Justice of the Supreme Court of the United States.

The occasion for my retirement arises from the affliction which I unexpectedly suffered last April. Since then I have undergone substantial improvement. High expectations were earlier expressed by my doctors that I would be able to resume my judicial duties with the beginning of the next Term of the Court, commencing October 1. However, they now advise me that the stepped-up therapy essential to that end involves hazards which might jeopardize the useful years they anticipate still lie ahead of me.

The Court should not enter its new Term with uncertainty as to whether I might later be able to return to unrestricted duty. To retain my seat on the basis of a diminished work schedule would not comport with my own philosophy or with the demands of the business of the Court. I am thus left with no choice but to regard my period of active service on the Court as having run its course.

I need hardly tell you, Mr. President, of the reluctance with which I leave the institution whose concerns have been the absorbing interest of my life. May I again convey to you my gratitude for your call upon me during the summer and for the solicitude you were kind enough to express.

With high respect and esteem,

Faithfully yours,
FELIX FRANKFURTER.

THE PRESIDENT,
The White House,
Washington, D. C.

THE WHITE HOUSE,
Washington, August 28, 1962

MY DEAR MR. JUSTICE FRANKFURTER:

Your retirement from regular active service on the Supreme Court ends a long and illustrious chapter in your life, and I understand well how hard a choice you have made. Along with all your host of friends I have followed with admiration your gallant and determined recovery, and I have shared the general hope that you would return soon to the Court's labors. From my own visit I know of your undiminished spirit and your still contagious zest for life. That you now take the judgment of the doctors and set it sternly against your own demanding standard of judicial effectiveness is characteristic, but it comes as an immediate disappointment.

Still, if you will allow it, I will say that there is also consolation in your decision. I believe it good for you as well as for the rest of us that you should now be free, in reflective leisure, for activities that are impossible in the demanding life of a Justice of the Supreme Court. You have been part of American public life for well over half a century. What you have learned of the meaning of our country is reflected, of course, in many hundreds of opinions, in thousands of your students, and in dozens of books and articles. But you have a very great deal still to tell us, and therefore I am glad to know that the doctors are telling you, in effect, not to retire, but only to turn to a new line of work, with new promise of service to the nation.

Meanwhile, I should like to offer to Mrs. Frankfurter and to you, for myself and for all Americans, our respectful gratitude for the character, courage, learning and judicial dedication with which you have served your country over the last twenty-three years.

Sincerely,
JOHN KENNEDY.

The Honorable FELIX FRANKFURTER,
Associate Justice,
Supreme Court of the United States,
Washington, D. C.

SUPREME COURT OF THE UNITED STATES.
Monday, March 1, 1965.

Present: MR. CHIEF JUSTICE WARREN, MR. JUSTICE BLACK, MR. JUSTICE DOUGLAS, MR. JUSTICE CLARK, MR. JUSTICE HARLAN, MR. JUSTICE BRENNAN, MR. JUSTICE STEWART, MR. JUSTICE WHITE, and MR. JUSTICE GOLDBERG.

THE CHIEF JUSTICE said:

"It is on a note of sadness that we open this session of the Court because, since we last met, our friend and Brother, Felix Frankfurter, has passed away.

"It was twenty-six years ago on January 30th that Mr. Justice Frankfurter took his seat on this Court. One week ago he died after a gallant fight for the restoration of the health which he had lost three years ago. In more than 23 years of service here, he had one of the longest and, without doubt, one of the most brilliant careers in the history of the Court.

"He was one of the most knowledgeable of men. He came to his high position with a combination of scholarship and public experience rarely equalled. As a scholar, teacher, public servant, man of letters, patron of the arts, and the confidant of Presidents, he had already made great contributions to the life of our Nation. But, notwithstanding his manifold activities, the law was always his preoccupation. He caught its spirit early in life, and to his very last day devoted himself fervently to its development under the Constitution which he revered.

"His death leaves a great void in the communities of scholars and jurists, but fortunately his written words, so pregnant with meaning, will be a heritage for all who love the law and believe in it as the sheet anchor of our civilization.

"We of the Supreme Court who knew him so well mourn his passing, both as our associate and friend, but we also know that his ebullient spirit would want us to get on with our always unfinished work."

Recommended Readings

The now-classic history of the Supreme Court is Charles Warren, *The Supreme Court in United States History*, 3 vols. (1922). Other historical accounts of the high Court include:

Haines, Charles G., *The Role of the Supreme Court in American Government and Politics, 1789-1835* (1961);

Haines, Charles G., and Sherwood, Foster H., *The Role of the Supreme Court in American Government and Politics, 1835-1864* (1957);

McCloskey, Robert G., *The American Supreme Court* (1960);

Pfeffer, Leo, *This Honorable Court: A History of the United States Supreme Court* (1965);

Pollak, Louis H., *The Constitution and the Supreme Court: A Documentary History* (1966);

Schwartz, Bernard, *The Supreme Court: Constitutional Revolution in Retrospect* (1957).

The Supreme Court also plays an important part in general constitutional histories, the most useful of which are:

Kelly, Alfred H., and Harbison, Winfred A., *The American Constitution, Its Origins and Development* (rev. ed., 1955);

McLaughlin, Andrew C., *A Constitutional History of the United States* (1935);

Schwartz, Bernard, *The Reigns of Power: A Constitutional History of the United States* (1963);

Swisher, Carl B., *American Constitutional Development* (2d ed., 1954).

Of particular interest to one concerned with the Supreme Court are the great commentaries which have not only explained but also significantly molded the work of the highest Court. Of these the most important are:

Story, Joseph, *Commentaries on the Constitution of the United States*, 3 vols. (1833);

Kent, James, *Commentaries on American Law*, 4 vols. (1826-1830);

Cooley, Thomas M., *A Treatise on the Constitutional Limitations Which Rest Upon the Legislative Power of the States of the American Union* (1868).

During the present century, the nearest equivalents (though nowhere near as consequential in their impact) have been:

Willoughby, Westel W., *The Constitutional Law of the United States,* 3 vols. (2d ed., 1929);

Corwin, Edward S., *The Constitution of the United States of America, Analysis and Interpretation* (1953).

The present writer has recently published the first two parts of a comprehensive commentary on the Constitution, entitled

A Commentary on the Constitution of the United States:

Part One, The Powers of Government (1963)
  Vol. I, *Federal and State Powers,*
  Vol. II, *The Powers of the President;*
Part Two, The Rights of Property (1965).

Part Three of this work, *Rights of the Person* (Vol. I, *Sanctity, Privacy, and Expression;* (Vol. II, *Equality, Belief, and Dignity*), will be published in 1968.

Index

Ableman v. Booth, 33, 34, 161
Adams, John, 15, 16, 70
Adams, John Quincy, 23
Agricultural Adjustment Act, 57, 61
agriculture, 54, 57, 61
Allgeyer v. Louisiana, 46, 129-131
American Communist Party, 68
arbitrary action, 51, 56

Baker v. Carr, 78-80, 162
Baldwin v. Missouri, 138-139
Bank of Augusta v. Earle, 31
Bill of Rights, 43, 72-73, 85-86
Brandeis, Louis D., Associate Justice, 55-56, 58, 81
Brewer, Justice, 52
Brown v. Board of Education, 74, 76, 158
Buchanan, James, 35

Chambers v. Florida, 151
Charles River Bridge v. Warren Bridge, 30-31, 117-121
Chase, Samuel, Associate Justice, impeachment of, 23-24
Chief Justice, duties of, 70-71
Child Labor case, 54-56, 61-62
Chisholm v. Georgia, 13-14
Circuit Courts, 13, 15
civil liberties, 43, 73, 76, 88
Civil War, 44, 65
Civil War cases, 37-38
Civilian Exclusion Orders, 66-67
Clark, Tom C., Associate Justice, 70, 167-174
Clay, Henry, 28
coal industry, 57-58, 61
Cohens v. Virginia, 22
Cold War, 67-69
commerce, 54-55, 57
commerce, interstate, 60-62, 76-77
commerce, regulation of, 25, 33
commerce clause, 25-26, 33, 53-55, 57-58, 61-62
Constitutional revolution, 59-60, 63, 84
Cooley v. Board Port Wardens, 33
Cooper v. Aaron, 75-76, 159-161

corporate development, 31
corporate personality, 31
corporations as "persons," 44-45
court appointed counsel, 77-78
court in operation, 167-174, 175-179
"court packing," 12, 42, 58-60, 80, 86, 140-145, 146-149
criminal justice, 77

Dartmouth College case, 31
Dennis v. United States, 68
Department of Conservation and Development v. Tate, 160
Derrington v. Plummer, 160
desegregation, 78
doctrinal foundations, judicial power for, 24-25
Douglas, William O., Associate Justice, 85-86
Dred Scott case, 20, 28, 34-36, 39, 41, 43, 122-125
due process, 44-46, 52, 53, 63-65, 73, 84-85
due process, substantive, 46, 50, 52-53, 63

economic theory, 52-53, 64-65
Eisenhower, Dwight, 70
Eleventh Amendment, 13
employment, minimum standards of, 53
equal civil rights, 43, 47
"equal population" principle, 79
equal protection, 47, 73-74, 77, 79
equality in facilities, 74
Escobedo v. Illinois, 78

Fair Labor Standards Act, 62
Farmers Loan & Trust Co. v. Minnesota, 138
federal system, arbiter of, 76
Field, Stephen J., Justice, 45, 46, 50
Fifteenth Amendment, 47, 74
Fletcher v. Peck, 21
Fourteenth Amendment, 43-46, 48, 50, 52, 64, 73-74, 77, 158
Frankfurter, Felix, Associate Justice, 46, 69, 76, 85, 180-186
freedom-of-contract formula, 53, 63

Fugitive Slave Act, 34
Gibbons v. Ogden, 24-26, 53
Gideon v. Wainwright, 77-78
Gomillion v. Lightfoot, 163
government and business, 44
Granger cases, 46
Grant, Ulysses S., 42
Griffin v. Illinois, 77, 150-152
Guinn v. United States, 163

habeas corpus, 37, 38, 66
Hamilton, Alexander, 12, 13
Harlan, John M., Associate Justice, 47-48, 52
Harrison, Robert, 13
Hepburn v. Griswold, 41-42
Hoadly, Bishop, 10
Holden v. Hardy, 137
Holmes, Oliver Wendell, Associate Justice, 10, 16, 51, 55-56, 58, 60, 63-64, 68, 136-139
Hughes, Charles E., Chief Justice, 9, 58, 59-60, 63, 71, 146-149

Illinois mudguard, 76-77
implied powers, doctrine of, 25 (*see also* necessary-and-proper cause)
Income Tax case, 50
indestructible Union, 38
industrial excesses, 52
injunctions in labor disputes, 53
Insular cases, 48
"interposition," 75
Interposition, Georgia Resolution, 153-158
interrogation and confessions, 78
Interstate Commerce Act, 53-54, 58

Jackson, Andrew, 27, 83, 113-116
Jackson, Robert H., Associate Justice, 58-59, 83, 88
Jacobson v. Massachusetts, 137
Japanese, evacuation of, 66-67
Jay, John, Chief Justice, 12, 14
Jefferson, Thomas, 14-15, 18, 23, 37, 110-112
Johnson, Andrew, 40-41, 126-128
Jones & Laughlin case, 60-61 (*see also NLRB v. Jones & Laughlin Steel Corp.*)
judicial power, structure of, 22
judicial review, 110-112
Judiciary Act of 1789, 11, 13, 18

Judiciary Act of 1801, 14-15
Judiciary Act of 1937, 59

Korematsu v. United States, 67

laissez-faire, 52, 55-57, 60, 84
Lane v. Wilson, 163
Legal Tender cases, 41-42
License cases, 32
Lincoln, Abraham, 36-38, 122-125
Liverpool & London & Globe Ins. Co. v. Assessors for the Parish of Orleans, 139
Lochner v. New York, 51-53, 55-56, 63, 136-138
loyalty-security programs, 68

McCardle case, 39-41, 126-128
McCulloch v. Maryland, 24-25, 41-42
McKane v. Durston, 152
McReynolds, James C., Associate Justice, 52
Madison, James, 18
manpower, conscription of, 65
manufacturing, 54-55, 57, 61
Marbury v. Madison, 18-21, 75, 104-109, 161
Marshall, John, Chief Justice, 10, 12, 16-22, 27, 28, 29, 32, 33, 35, 62, 70, 71, 72, 75, 83, 88, 99-103
Marshall Court, 16-26, 27, 28, 31, 53, 54, 162
Martin v. Hunter's Lessee, 21
maximum hours, 62
Midnight Judges Bill, 15, 18
military arrests and trials, 39-40
Milligan case, 39
minimum wages, 53, 60, 62
mining, 54, 57, 61
minorities, rights of, 73
Miranda v. Arizona, 78
Missouri Compromise, 35
Mr. Dooley, 49, 83, 132-135
Morris, Gouverneur, 15

nation-state relationship, 44
National Labor Relations Act, 60-61
National Labor Relations Board v. Jones & Laughlin Steel Corp., 60
National Industrial Recovery Act, 57

KF8742
.S3
1979

Schwartz

A basic history of the U.S.
   Supreme Court

necessary-and-proper clause, 24
Negro, 35-36, 43, 45-48, 73-75
New Deal cases, 57-62, 83-84
Nixon v. Herndon, 163
Northern Securities Co. v. United States, 137

Otis v. Parker, 137
average jurists, 58

Pennsylvania v. Board of Directors of City Trusts of Philadelphia, 160
Plessy v. Ferguson, 46-48, 74
police power, 32
Prize cases, 36-37
production, 53
property, mobilized, 65

racial discrimination, 73-74
rate-fixing legislation, 46
reapportionment, 78-79
"reasonable man," 56
Reconstruction period, 39, 41
review power, 19-20, 23, 27
review power over national government, 22, 24, 33, 34, 59
review power over states, 21-22, 24, 33-34, 46, 51-52, 76
Reynolds v. Sims, 79-80, 162-166
right to organize collectively, 60
rights, community, 29-30, 32, 85
rights, personal, 29, 32, 44, 51, 56, 72-73, 84, 86
rights, property, 29-30, 44-46, 56, 72-73, 84
Roosevelt, Franklin D., 12, 57-60, 140-145

saboteurs, 65-66
Safe Deposit & Trust Co. v. Virginia, 138
Santa Clara County v. Southern Pacific Railroad, 44
security, 68, 69
segregation, 47, 71-72, 74, 75
"separate but equal" doctrine, 74
Shelley v. Kraemer, 160
Sherman Anti-Trust Act, 54
Ex parte Siebold, 163
Sixteenth Amendment, 50
Slaughter-House cases, 45
Smith Act, 68
Smith v. Texas, 160
state sovereignty, 75
Sterling v. Constantin, 161

Stone, Harlan F., Chief Justice, 66
Story, Joseph, Associate Justice, 22, 27, 31, 82
Stuart v. Laird, 15
substantive law, 71-72
suffrage, right of, 79
supremacy clause, 24

Taft, William, Chief Justice, 14
Taney, Roger B., Chief Justice, 27-35, 75, 83
Taney Court, 27-34, 162
territories, 49
territories, incorporated and unincorporated, 49
territory, residence in, 35-36
Texas v. White, 38
Thirteenth Amendment, 47
Tocqueville, Alexis de, 10
transcripts, free, 77

uniform case-law, 38
United States v. Classic, 163
United States v. Darby, 62
United States v. E. C. Knight Co., 54
United States v. Mosley, 162
United States v. Peters, 161
United States v. Saylor, 163

Vietnam conflict, 37
Vinson, Frederick M., Chief Justice, 72
Vinson Court, 72
Virginia v. Rives, 160

Waite, Morrison R., Chief Justice, 44
war, declaration of, 37
Warren, Earl, Chief Justice, 39, 70, 71, 79
Warren Court, 70-80, 87
Washington, George, 14, 27, 53, 91-93, 97-98
Webster, Daniel, 27
Welfare State, 85
Wheeler v. Sohmer, 139
white primaries, 47, 74
Wilson, James, Associate Justice, 14
World War II, 65, 84
worker protection, 52

Ex parte Yarbrough, 162
yellow-dog contracts, 53
Yick Wo v. Hopkins, 151